THE FRAMEWORK OF CRIMINAL JUSTICE

THE FRAMEWORK OF CRIMINAL JUSTICE

MICHAEL KING

CROOM HELM LONDON

© 1981 Michael King
Croom Helm Ltd, 2-10 St John's Road, London SW11

British Library Cataloguing in Publication Data

King, Michael
   The framework of criminal justice.
   1. Police magistrates — England
   2. Criminal justice, Administration of — England
   I. Title
   345'.42'05   KD8309

   ISBN 0-7099-0430-4
   ISBN 0-7099-1500-4 (Pbk)

Reproduced from copy supplied
printed and bound in Great Britain
by Billing and Sons Limited
Guildford, London, Oxford, Worcester

Contents

'Every human institution (justice included) will stretch a little, if only you pull it the right way.'

Wilkie Collins

Acknowledgements

I should like to thank Andrew Ashworth and my colleagues William Twining and Sol Picciotto for their helpful comments on various parts of this book. My thanks also to Al Katz at Buffalo for some useful ideas in the early stages of the book's conception. Finally, much of the credit for Chapter 3 must go to Malcolm Nicholson's hard work as my research assistant, although the final version with any errors it might contain is entirely my responsibility.

Understanding the Criminal Justice Process

The popular image of the criminal justice system fostered by fiction writers, films and the broadcasting media is of courtroom drama following courtroom drama as lawyers for the prosecution and defence relentlessly do battle with one another. Policemen catch criminals through brilliant detective work; witnesses break down under cross-examination and justice is done. Unfortunately, reality rarely lives up to this image, as anyone who has any experience of magistrates' courts will testify. Most defendants have confessed to the police and so made unnecessary all but the most basic detective work. Full-blooded trials in these courts are a comparative rarity. Most of the court's time is spent deciding what should happen to people who either have pleaded or will eventually plead guilty. Yet, it is not by chance that the quest for truth and justice personified in the popular images of the detective who always 'gets his man' and the defence lawyer who always 'wins his case' have become part of the mythology of criminal justice. In a society which claims to value truth and justice we would all like to believe that it is these values which predominate in those social institutions which determine who is guilty and who should be punished. However, if this were the case, there would be no need for this book. One could simply accept as reality the romanticised versions of criminal justice that abound in the popular culture. In concentrating attention upon the usual rather than the exceptional, the ordinary rather than the extraordinary, in focusing upon the daily routine business of policemen, lawyers, court clerks, probation officers and magistrates as they process all those defendants who plead guilty, one of the things I hope to show is how the concepts of truth and justice, far from providing any absolute standards for the conduct of the actors, are often used in a rhetorical manner to legitimate the pursuit of institutional and social objectives. These objectives may well appear just to those who strive to achieve them or who sympathise with them and the version of reality presented in order to attain these objectives may appear to them to be truthful. However, to those who do not share or sympathise with these objectives, or who positively oppose them, that version of reality might seem a complete distortion of the truth and the outcome of the case a total perversion of justice.

To a large degree the popular myths concerning criminal justice were, until quite recently, reflected in the specialist literature. Textbooks on the English legal system by focusing their attention on the rules and regulations governing the system's operation tended to present a totally idealised account of the criminal justice process. Similarly, the staple diet for aspiring criminal lawyers has been, and still is in many law departments and colleges, the criminal law and the rules of evidence, with little or no consideration of police interrogation practices, the role of probation officers, the legal aid system or the sentencing powers of the magistrates' courts. Perhaps this is not so surprising when one considers that until the late sixties few practising lawyers ever set foot in the lower courts and when they did it was usually in circumstances far removed from the routine handling of minor offenders set on pleading guilty. The growth of criminal legal aid and the emergence of duty solicitor schemes changed all that. Alongside these reforms there began to appear a body of literature which was specifically concerned with the plight of defendants. They ranged from studies of the bail, legal aid and sentencing decisions in the lower courts to interviews with prisoners about their experiences at the hands of the police and magistrates and analyses of the roles of courtroom 'professionals' or the use of courtroom language. Much of this work was inspired by a genuine concern for the poor, the inadequate, the underdogs of society. It found expression both in a liberal reformist approach which attempted to identify the failures and injustices of the present system and the application of a neo-Marxist ideology which saw the criminal justice process in class conflict terms, with defendants as the representatives of an oppressed class and those who prosecuted, represented and sentenced them as instruments of repression. For reasons which should become clear during the course of this study neither of these approaches has proved entirely satisfactory. Moreover, the ideological differences between them, seemingly irreconcilable, has tended to divide researchers and writers from both law and the social sciences into two distinct camps. Theory has become almost synonymous with neo-Marxist theory, while the task of reforming the system has proceeded in a pragmatic, piecemeal manner with very little regard to social policy and the broad objectives of a criminal justice system. I make no claims to offer in the ensuing pages a peace formula to reconcile these two camps, but what this book does attempt to do is to provide a coherent analysis of the workings of the criminal justice system using both ideological and strategic perspectives rather than applying one to the exclusion of the other.

What it also attempts to do is to develop a framework for the understanding of the relationship between rules and behaviour within the criminal justice system, for without such a framework it is fruitless to talk of reforming the system by changing the formal rules. In the past there has been a tendency, particularly among lawyers, to assume that changes in the law and legal procedures will result automatically in desired changes in the way the system operates in practice. Too often the good intentions of reformers have been thwarted by the capacity of interest groups to interpret and adapt would-be reforms so that they fit neatly into existing patterns of behaviour. On other occasions reforming the rules has led to unforeseen and undesired changes in the behaviour of those who operate the system. More recently some sociological researchers have proceeded on the basis that the only valid subject for study and analysis is the behaviour of the actors. The law and the rules of evidence and procedure, as far as they are worth considering at all, merely legitimate the conduct of the actors. Adopting one of these approaches to the exclusion of the other not only limits the capacity for understanding how the present system works, but it also tends to give a false impression, either over-optimistic or unduly pessimistic, as to what it is possible to achieve through reform of the formal rules. I have attempted in this book to bring an extra dimension to this particular problem. After analysing the routine processes of criminal justice in terms of their possible social objectives, I have gone on to look at the process of law reform in an attempt to examine the response of politicians and civil servants to proposals for changing the formal rules.

It is necessary at this stage to explain why I have chosen to limit this study to guilty pleaders in magistrates' courts rather than tackling the whole of the criminal justice system. The principle reason for selecting only those defendants who plead guilty lies in the fact, already mentioned, that it is only a very small proportion of defendants who contest the case against them. Through sheer weight of numbers, therefore, it is these defendants or rather the problems in dealing with them that tend to dominate the criminal justice system, at least at the magistrates' court. It would, of course, have been possible to consider all defendants whose cases ended at the magistrates' courts. The problem with this approach, however, is that the element of conflict engendered by that small proportion of defendants who plead not guilty would tend to attract much more interest than either their number or their importance to the objectives of this study would justify. The routine processing of defendants before and during the court hearing would tend to vanish from view as the reader concentrated his attention on issues of guilt and innocence, the very quest for truth and justice which characterises the popular image of the courts and detracts from any consciousness of the system as it operates for the majority of defendants.

There are three reasons why I have chosen not to go beyond the magistrates' court stage. In the first place the English system of criminal justice is so organised that a clear division exists between magistrates' courts and Crown Courts. In the magistrates' court the majority of defendants plead guilty, are unrepresented by lawyers and are sentenced by part-time lay justices. Of the comparatively few defendants who reach the Crown Court, by contrast, most start at least with the intention of contesting their cases; almost all are represented by barristers and those who are found guilty are sentenced by professional judges. Although it is not directly relevant to guilty pleaders, it is also worth noting that in the magistrates' courts most contested cases are tried by the lay justices, while at the Crown Court it is jurors who determine the factual issues and judges who interpret the law. These fundamental differences make it difficult to generalise about the criminal justice process, for the way things are done in the Crown Court is often very different from the magistrates' court. One would need two separate studies in order to do justice to the complexities of the two systems. Having made this point, however, it is also worth commenting that on the more general level of social theory concerning the relationship of the courts to society at large, rather than that of detailed descriptive evidence, many of the points concerning the nature and purpose of the process which I shall be making during the course of this study of magistrates' courts could apply equally to the Crown Court, or for that matter, to the Court of Appeal.

Secondly, as a solicitor, it is with the magistrates' courts that I am most familiar. Indeed, I have practised off and on in magistrates' courts in the London and the Midlands for more than ten years. Furthermore, almost all the research studies I have conducted have been on the subject of magistrates' courts. Although, admittedly, it is possible for social researchers to write interesting studies on aspects of the social system which they have observed from the outside, such studies often resemble slow journalism rather than providing any penetrating insights into the phenomena and observation. I would suggest that such insights are much more likely to come from people who have acquired first-hand knowledge and experience over fairly long periods of the phenomena under analysis.

Finally, few other English institutions have been subjected to so much adverse criticism over the past 25 years as have the magistrates' courts. These criticisms have been directed against almost every aspect of the courts and against the constitution and characteristics of the magistracy. The courts have been taken to task for their archaic buildings, their lack of facilities for lawyers and the public, the apparent police domination of proceedings and the long delays experienced by many defendants. The magistrates have been attacked for their class and racial exclusivity, their lack of training, their lack of legal knowledge, the harshness of their decisions, the 'softness' of their decisions, their lack of concern for the victim and their lack of direct experience of the living conditions and mores of those on whom they pass judgement. They and their clerks have also been severely criticised by different commentators for their arbitrary handling of bail and legal aid applications, for the perfunctory manner in which they reach some decisions and the inordinate length of time taken in reaching others, for the variations and inconsistencies in their decisions, for their arrogant and humiliating treatment of defendants in the courtroom.

Often the criticisms are the spontaneous responses to specific situations. But even where they are the result of long and detailed studies of magistrates' courts by careful researchers or lawyers and magistrates with considerable experience of their operation, it is almost unknown for the critic to consider what social function magistrates' courts are performing and to relate this criticism in any specific way to a failure in the achievement of functional objectives. Almost always these functions are assumed rather than spelt out and almost always the assumptions reflect the ideological perspective of the critic, be he a policeman, a politician, a defence lawyer, a sociologist or a probation officer. The validity of any criticism is relative only to the objectives the critic believes the courts should be seeking to achieve.

Moreover, these criticisms have tended to emphasise the uniqueness of the magistrates' courts as social institutions. If they are not functioning properly, then the explanation must lie, for example, in their amateurishness or in the fact that they are too close to police stations or lack proper facilities for lawyers. The corollary of such criticisms is that if these matters were only put right, if, for example, magistrates were paid and trained, if the courts were separated from police stations and housed in modern buildings, then all would be well for criminal justice. Unfortunately, as we shall see, things are much more complicated than that. Magistrates' courts might be uniquely English (and Welsh) institutions, but their uniqueness should not mask the fact that they share much in common with many other institutions within our society. They exist in the same cultural, economic and political environment as these other institutions and cannot therefore satisfactorily be understood by regarding them as if they were located in some sterile social vacuum, isolated from everything else that goes on in society by the twin ideologies of justice and community participation. In this study I have tried through the use of process models as a method of analysis to capture some of the unique properties of magistrates' justice while at the same time relating what happens in the criminal justice process to the wider social structure and to those economic and political forces affecting the form and operation of institutions within our society.

The following short summary of the ensuing chapters should help to give the reader an idea of the approach that this book takes and of the sort of issues it covers. With the exception of Chapter 3, which may be omitted by lawyers and others familiar with the law, the book should be read from cover to cover in the order in which it was written, rather than 'dipped into'. Since the chapters and sections of chapters are for the most part interdependent, the 'dipping' reader is almost certain to miss the main thrust of the analysis.

Chapter 2: Theoretical Approaches to Criminal Justice

This chapter sets out the theoretical basis for the subsequent analysis of the criminal justice process. It explains the need for theories and the advantage of using theoretical models as a method of analysis. It also describes and defines the six process models to be employed in the present study.

Chapter 3: The Formal Process

This chapter summarises the formal rule structure within which the participants to the criminal justice process in magistrates' courts operate. It is not intended as a definitive statement of the law, and should not be used as such. Rather, it is designed to give those readers unfamiliar with the law some understanding of the way in which the relevant legislation, case law and procedural rules set out the powers available to the participants and the restraints on their actions. It also considers the statistical evidence that is available concerning the operation of these formal rules.

Chapter 4: Scenes in the Criminal Justice Process

As the title suggests, this chapter describes eight scenes occurring between the arrest of a suspect for questioning by the police and the sentencing of a defendant by the court. These descriptions are supported by evidence, both statistical and anecdotal. During the course of these descriptions, it gives an account of the relationship between the suspect/defendant and the regular participants to the criminal justice process, policemen, lawyers, probation officers, court clerks and magistrates.

Chapter 5: Making Sense of the System

Here the process models described in Chapter 2 are applied systematically to the evidence, both formal and informal, as to the system's operation presented in Chapters 3 and 4. The chapter ends with a series of impressions gained from the analysis which carry implications for the understanding of the criminal justice process and for its reform.

Chapter 6: Getting the System Right: The Process of Law Reform

The final chapter examines two recent attempts to reform the criminal justice process, the Bail Act 1976 and two sections of the Criminal Law Act 1977. The chapter compares an ideal model of law reform based on principles of rationality, impartiality and democracy with the actual process of law reform as it occurred in these two examples. The book ends with a concluding section which draws attention to the similarities and connections between the criminal justice system and the machinery for reforming that system. It explains how real reform must ultimately depend upon real understanding of the criminal justice system, the effects of the formal rules and of the economic and political movements which underlie both the processes of criminal justice and law reform.

Theoretical Approaches to Criminal Justice

1. Social Theories

Throughout this book I shall use the term 'theory' to refer to many general principles or set of principles formulated to explain the events in the world or relations between such events. The theories I shall refer to are social theories, that is those theories which attempt to account for social events. Not only do such theories provide explanations for past social behaviour, but they also offer predictions as to the future. Social policies are based upon theories of social behaviour, since those who formulate the policies make certain assumptions about the policies and the social objectives they seek to achieve through political actions derived from such policies. To take a well-documented example, policy emphasises the importance of free education from kindergarten through to university level, the desired objective being not merely that education should be free to anybody who wishes to take advantage of it but, more importantly, that free education should bring about social mobility and equality of opportunity. The casual relationship between the concepts of free education and those of social mobility and equality of opportunity is based upon a theoretical assumption about the way society works.

Although many of the social policies put into effect by political parties are related to explicit social theories, this is not always the case. Policies may be implicit or intuitive or they may be pragmatic, in which case no *a priori* general principles or set of principles have been set out which explain and predict the relationship between the political acts and their objectives. This does not mean that these policies have no theoretical underpinning, but merely that the terms of the theory have not been made explicit. Often political commentators will, in the absence of any clearly defined policy objectives, speculate about the motivations of particular politicians or political parties, basing their speculations upon their interpretations of various political actions. In other words, they attempt to construct a theory which will explain social policies. This is a very similar exercise to the one undertaken for much of the remainder of this book, for it will examine in the light of the available evidence theories which attempt to explain the way in which the legal process affecting guilty pleaders operates. From this exercise it should be possible to construct a framework for interpreting the relationship between social policy and the actual practice of the law in magistrates' courts.

All of the theories discussed in this chapter could be described as 'explicit theories', in that the general principles or set of principles which each of them encompasses have been set out in a formal or semi-formal manner by different writers. This does not mean to say that everyone who is responsible for the operation of the criminal justice process in magistrates' courts would have read one or more of these theories and will consciously be applying its principles in his actions and decisions. It is much more likely that these principles will in varying degrees correspond to what the various actors regard as 'common sense', 'human nature', or 'the way things work'. In other words they may well be incorporated in the taken-for-granted, conventional wisdoms of the actors.

Yet it may be that some of the ideas to be discussed are far removed from these common-sense notions or conventional wisdoms. This does not make them any the less valid as possible explanations of social events. The test of their validity is not whether practising lawyers or policemen agree with them but the extent to which they offer useful insights into the operation of the criminal justice system in magistrates' courts.

We shall return later in this chapter to discuss the relationship between the different theoretical perspectives which we shall be applying. Before doing so, let us consider the value of using theories in the analysis of social phenomena.

2. Why Use Theories?

A fundamental dilemma facing many social scientists is that 'social reality' exists only in the mind of that society's members. It is real for them, because they have, through the process of socialisation, acquired a conceptual framework which allows them to attribute meanings and values to social phenomena and thus to interpret events occurring in their social world. One cannot, for example, see, hear or feel a legal system. One may, of course, see a courtroom where groups of people gather together; one may watch them moving and hear them talking, but this tells the observer little about the social situation and nothing about the institution, its rules, the assumptions of the participants and their attitude towards their roles, or about the power or authority structure which allows one group of people to make decisions affecting the future action of other groups. It is the meaning of social phenomena which is important to the social scientists rather than mere physical characteristics. While he should approach each new social situation without prior assumptions or preconceptions, this is impossible, since his own socialisation has caused him to attach meanings and values to the social phenomena he is investigating.

Another complication is that members of the same society do not necessarily draw similar meanings, make identical assumptions, or attach the same values to social phenomena. Socialisation is not merely a matter of stamping 'reality' upon the mind of each new member of society. In internalising social reality the individual imposes his own interpretation upon events. As the individual matures he defines his social experiences in a repetitive manner and his internalised model becomes increasingly less susceptible to change and adjustment; it becomes, in effect, the taken-for-granted world of that individual. Social researchers are not immune from such processes. Their values and beliefs will influence the framework in which they operate, including attitudes towards their subject, the questions they ask, the way in which they ask them and the interpretations placed upon the answers they obtain.

Some have naively attempted to escape from these problem by limiting their presentation of data to description. These writers may either portray aspects of proceedings in one court or a number of specific courts and offer these portraits as being typical and comprehensive of behaviour in magistrates' courts in general.[1] They are still, however, presenting a subjective account of the way the courts operate, since there is no such thing as pure description of a social system. Any description involves interpretation and selectivity. What is selected and why it is interpreted will depend to a large extent upon the values and preconceptions which the observer brings to the social situation. The social scientist using descriptive approaches usually fails to make explicit his own theoretical perspective. In the same way that different readers may feel the need to attach varying degrees of credibility to the differing reports of the same political event which appear in different newspapers depending usually upon the extent to which the reader shares the journalist's political perspective, readers of social research also face a similar problem. For them, however, the problem is made more difficult by the fact that researchers, unlike some newspapers, do not usually fly any political or ideological colours. Therefore, the reader usually has to read between the lines in order to make assumptions about the writer's ideological perspective to enable him to judge the value and validity of the study. These assumptions, accurate or not, are necessary for the reader to fill in the gaps left by the researcher.

The use of statistics, unless related to some explicit theoretical model, does not in itself represent an advance over the descriptive approach, unless to give it a specious aura of validity through the presentation of figures and percentages. The limitation of much recent legal research in the area of criminal justice is that it has tended to be either atheoretical or based upon an implicit model of the legal process which has proved altogether too simple. Much of the research into the effects of legal representation in magistrates' courts has, for example, consisted merely of statistical comparisons between the outcomes of those represented and those unrepresented. Such studies are based on the implicit assumption that in the main there are no differences between represented and unrepresented defendants other than the fact of legal representation. It may well be the case, however, that a defendant who is convinced of his own innocence will be more likely to seek a solicitor's help than one who is pleading not guilty in order to avoid losing face and admitting that his story to the police was a fabric of lies. It is possible to produce a theoretical model incorporating the hypothesis that the strength of the defendant's conviction in his own innocence is a major factor in determining the lengths he is prepared to go to and the risks he is prepared to take in proving his innocence in court. A different theoretical hypothesis might be that middle-class defendants, who appreciate the value of professional help and are more likely to consult a lawyer, are at the same time better able to articulate their story in front of the magistrates or judge and may for this reason stand a greater chance of acquittal. In other words, factors which bring the defendant to decide upon taking legal representation may also be important in determining whether he is convicted. Such explanations have been ignored entirely by most researchers on this subject, who, because they operate from a narrow, 'legal reformist' theoretical perspective, have tended to concern themselves rather with simple comparisons between the results obtained in court by represented defendants. The method chosen in this study to avoid the errors and distortions that may result from total subjectivity or from the use of one ideological viewpoint to the exclusion of all others is to employ a multi-theoretical approach. This somewhat pretentious sounding method is in fact very simple to explain.

If the question 'what is the purpose of the criminal justice process?' were put to a broad cross-section of the population it would probably yield a wide variety of answers. The answers would no doubt reflect different levels of knowledge and intelligence as well as the different ideological perspectives of the respondents. The various theories of the court's social function set out in the column I of Figure 1 also offer a broad spectrum of ideological perspectives. They have been proposed by different writers to explain the role of the courts in our society. Numbers one to three may be seen as reflecting in a general way the attitudes of the regular participants in the magistrates' court process as well as the uses that may be made of these courts to achieve certain policy objectives. Numbers four to six, on the other hand, represent different social roles for the courts as proposed in sociological literature. These two groups are not, however, totally unconnected, as we shall see when we examine the relationship between them. Let us first, however, look at the process models and the features derived from them, as set out in columns II and III.

3. Process Models

From the theoretical, social policy level we may move to the level of 'process models' in column II. These models are derived from the social policy functions that are implicit in the theoretical approaches. As in the physical and social sciences, the term model is used here to denote a hypothetical but coherent scheme for testing the evidence. However, our concern in this study will be not just to test the validity of the process models as accurate accounts of the operation of the criminal justice system as it relates to guilty pleaders in magistrates' courts. In addition, we shall be attempting to construct a comprehensive picture of the system's operation in order to discover how successfully it promotes the social policy functions set out in column I of Figure 1.

Furthermore, the six 'process models' may be seen as corresponding to the attitudes of six different people each looking from the vantage point which they believe will give them the best perspective over the system. Admittedly it would be difficult to find six people each of whose attitudes reflected precisely the features of one of the individual models and excluded features from any of the others. They would have to be ideal rather than real people. Nevertheless, imagine for example

Figure 1: Theoretical Models and their Features

I Social Function	II Process Model	III Features of Court
1. Justice	Due Process Model	(a) Equality between parties (b) Rules protecting defendant against error (c) Restraint of arbitrary power (d) Presumption of innocence
2. Punishment	Crime Control Model	(a) Disregard of legal controls (b) Implicit presumption of guilt (c) High conviction rate (d) Unpleasantness of experience (e) Support for police
3. Rehabilitation	Medical Model (diagnosis, prediction and treatment selection)	(a) Information collecting procedures (b) Individualisation (c) Treatment presumption (d) Discretion of decision-makers (e) Expertise of decision-makers or advisers (f) Relaxation of formal rules
4. Management of crime and criminals	Bureaucratic Model	(a) Independence from political considerations (b) Speed and efficiency (c) Importance of and acceptance of records (d) Minimisation of conflict (e) Minimisation of expense (f) Economical division of labour
5. Denunciation and degradation	Status Passage Model	(a) Public shaming of defendant (b) Court values reflecting community values (c) Agents' control over the process
6. Maintenance of class domination	Power Model	(a) Reinforcement of class values (b) Alienation and suppression of defendant (c) Deflection of attention from issues of class conflict (d) Differences between judges and judged (e) Paradoxes and contradictions between rhetoric and performance

the approach of the victim of a serious crime. He wishes to see the offender punished and deterred from further offences. Now compare that approach with that of a court administrator, whose major concern is the efficient running of the system, clearing the work-load for the day and avoiding any unnecessary delays.

Although observing the same case both these people have very different views of the court's operation. The one looks to the magistrates to revenge his loss or injury against the perpetrators of the crime and to compensate him, the victim, while the other looks at his watch and wonders how long the case is going to last and whether the morning list will be completed by one o'clock. Similarly, 'ideal' observers whose perspectives derive from the different formal models of the court's function set out in the first column of Figure 1 are likely not only to have very different expectations concerning the way the court should operate; they would also look for different features in the court's operation. A person who believes, therefore, that the court should act primarily to rehabilitate offenders will select very different aspects of the criminal justice process in magistrates' courts and will evaluate them differently to one who regards the court's only function as one of punishment.

Column III of Figure 1 sets out those features of each process model which ideally one would expect to find in the court's operation were the court applying exclusively that particular model. Thus, for example, by answering the question 'What presumptions are made by the court about the defendant?', it should be possible to identify which of the process models most appropriately reflects the actual operation of courts. Unfortunately, however, things are not quite as simple as that, for different interpretations of social events are not necessarily mutually exclusive. A presumption of guilt may, for example, exist side by side with the presumption that treatment or status reduction is required. Moreover, the court's role may change according to the type of defendant who appears in the dock or according to the nature of the hearing. A different theoretical model may, therefore, be more appropriate for explaining the court's actions in a contested bail application as opposed to a sentencing hearing following a guilty plea. These problems do not, however, detract from the value of examining aspects of the court's process successively from different theoretical perspectives, for it is through defining the limits of these theoretical models and the relationships between them that a more complete understanding of the operation of the magistrates' courts may be achieved. Let us now look at each of the process models in turn, its relationship to the social policy perspective from which it is derived and the features within the system that we would expect to find corresponding to the model's operation.

4. The Six Theories and Their Models

Justice and Due Process

The primary function of the magistrates' court, according to this perspective, is to resolve conflicts that arise between individual citizens and between the state and the citizens. The state acts as guardian of the peace to maintain the rule of law and to prevent private vengeance against the alleged perpetrators of crime. In so doing the state takes on the role of accuser and must prove that the defendant has broken the criminal law. The police representing the state and the accused are the parties to the dispute. Thus, since the individual must be safeguarded against the exercise of arbitrary power by the state, he is provided with legal protection and the onus is on the state to prove its case against him. The magistrates' court is one forum within the system of institutionalised justice for arbitrating between the two sides, while the magistrates are the impartial arbiters. The application of this view of the social function of the magistrates as independent arbitrators is clearly appropriate to those cases where the defendant contests the charges against him. However, it may also be applicable to bail hearings where the defendant is opposing the police's request to hold him in custody pending trial and, less obviously, to the sentencing process, where the court's decision-making may be seen as balancing the demands of the state for public protection and the maintenance of law and order against the individual's interests in preserving his liberty and minimising the extent of state intervention in his life.

Herbert Packer, the late American legal scholar, proposed that the whole of the criminal justice system could be interpreted, not so much as a battle between the prosecution and defence, but as a conflict and thus a balancing of two competing value systems or models, those of due process and crime control.[2] The crime control model, as the name suggests, has as the primary objective of the system the repression of criminal conduct, while the due process model emphasises the possibility of errors in informal, non-adjudicative fact-finding activities such as identification parades and confessions. In order to avoid and eliminate as far as possible such errors it insists upon adherence to the formal rules and adjudicative adversary processes. Central to the model are the presumption of innocence and the inviolability of legal rules governing the police powers and the admissibility of evidence. The function of the courts in promoting justice and the due process model are clearly related. Since fairness and justice are seen as the all-important ideals, the due process approach attempts to enshrine in pre-

hearing and courtroom procedures the principles of fairness and
protection of the individual against the power of the state. There
must, for example, be equality between prosecution and defence and
a defendant must be afforded every opportunity possible to clear his
name and discredit the case against him. Packer thus likens the due
process model of the criminal justice process to

> an obstacle course. Each of its successive stages is designed to present
> formidable impediments to carrying the accused any further along
> in the process . . . It resembles a factory that has to devote a sub-
> stantial part of its input to quality control. This necessarily cuts
> down on quantitative output.[3].

The values implicit in this model of the criminal justice process run
contrary to the utilitarian view that the welfare of the greatest number
is all important and that to inflict suffering on an individual is a permissible evil provided that sufficient benefits accrue to the remainder
of the population. Rather they emphasise the primacy of the individual's interests where conflict exists between the individual and the
state even if this entails limiting state power and reducing its effectiveness to control crime. Of course it may be necessary to punish and even
incarcerate offenders once their guilt or dangerousness has been proved
according to stringent criteria, but strict controls should be imposed
upon the state in the exercise of its role of accuser, since the arbitrary
or excessive use of state power is perceived as a worse evil than the
failure to convict and punish every offender. Moreover, if the courts
are to promote social justice then they must show that they are themselves institutions where a person can expect a fair hearing. They must
also be seen as places where a person who has been found guilty of a
crime receives a just penalty, that is one that reflects the seriousness of
the offence, his blameworthiness, and the harm caused to his victims.

In England the due process approach is associated with the attitudes
of the legal profession particularly those involved in defence work and
with the aims of such organisations as Justice and the National Council
for Civil Liberties. It has motivated much of the 'liberal reformist'
research into and criticisms of criminal justice in this country.

Punishment and Crime Control

According to this perspective, the primary function of the criminal
courts is to punish offenders and, in punishing them, to control crime.
The traditional justifications for punishment are retribution and

deterrence. The retributionist position is that it is morally right to punish offenders, because in punishing them the law gives expression to the feelings of hatred and disgust which people experience when confronted with crime. It ritualises and at the same time legitimates these feelings and in doing so both enhances moral standards within society and restrains those who might otherwise choose to take the law into their own hands by seeking vengeance against the offender. Thus, 'the criminal law', according to Sir James Stephen, an avid supporter of retribution, 'stands in the same relation to the passion of revenge as marriage does to the sexual passion'. The criminal should be punished according to his deserts. This is measured by estimating first, the amount of harm caused by his crime and secondly, the extent that he was to blame for causing that harm. This contrasts with the second of the two justifications, deterrence, which sees the role of punishment as dissuading both the offender from committing future criminal acts and potential offenders from imitating the offender's crime. Advocates of deterrence would argue that fear of the consequences is the principal reason why people do not commit crimes. Those who are caught must, therefore, be punished in a manner which will deter them from further crime; this is known as 'special deterrence'. At the same time, the court must have regard to effects of its sentence on the rest of the community, known as 'general deterrence'. Clearly the effectiveness of both special and general deterrence varies according to the individual involved and the type of offence. Moreover, the general deterrent effect may work indirectly in that the court's punishment is an expression of disapproval of certain forms of behaviour and the severity of the punishment an indication of the extent of this disapproval. These evaluations of behaviour may feed back into the social system, defining for society's members what is and what is not permissible.

Central to both the retribution and deterrence aspects of punishment is the assumption that people are fully responsible for their behaviour. Even where the criminal acts were the result of the defendant's loss of self-control, the punishment approach assumes that he made a conscious choice in allowing himself to reach such a state or to be exposed to such a situation where his control over himself might be weakened.

According to this perspective, the criminal courts may be seen and may see themselves as guardians of law and order in more senses than one. In the first place, they must punish the defendant for his infractions of the law. In doing so they condemn his acts and uphold the authority of the police in bringing him to justice. Secondly, they must keep an eye on the effects of their actions on the world outside the courtroom. Any failure to punish certain crimes or to punish them with sufficient severity might be interpreted as a sign of weakness and these bad examples may lead others to engage in anti-social behaviour in the belief that even if they are caught, the law will do nothing to them. If this pattern persists, so it is argued, it might eventually lead to a massive breakdown in law and order, particularly for crimes associated with poverty and white-collar crimes where people stand to gain materially from their acts.

In order to fulfil this role the criminal justice process must itself demonstrate that crime does not pay. A high acquittal rate, for example, would result in the public believing either that the police were arresting and charging a large number of innocent people or that too many criminals were 'getting away with it'. In both cases the courts would be failing to play their part in controlling crime, for, in the first case, the efficiency and integrity of the police would be undermined and, secondly, potential criminals might well be encouraged to commit offences by the knowledge that even if they were caught, it is unlikely that they would be convicted. Moreover, sentences which had little or no impact on defendants would be likely to have similar effects, for the police would soon become demoralised if they felt that their efforts in investigating the crime and catching the criminal resulted in no action from the courts, and potential offenders would be encouraged by the knowledge that even if they were convicted, they would not suffer any real punishment.

Although it is true that the crime control model may involve more than simple deterrence of the offenders and potential offenders, the theory and the process model are closely related and a model of the criminal justice process designed on the assumption that crime control is the only or paramount function of that process would include identical features to a model having deterrence only as its objective. These features which are set out in the third column of Figure 1 include a high conviction rate and support of the police which have already been mentioned. The 'disregard of legal controls' refers to the tendency for the imposition of formal rules of procedure and evidence designed for the defendant's protection to be perceived as having little value but rather as presenting obstacles in the way of the processing of defendents or 'ceremonial rituals which do not advance the progress of a case'.[4]

The 'implicit presumption of guilt' which will characterise any court proceeding based upon a crime control model is based upon the prior presumption that the police may be relied on to bring to court only those who are probably guilty and to screen out the probably innocent. While the presumption of innocence is a 'direction to officials about how they are to proceed' and 'not a prediction of outcome', the presumption of guilt is 'purely and simply a prediction of outcome'.[5] It may well, however, play an important part in shaping the atmosphere of the court and the attitude of officials towards the defendant. If it is believed that almost all defendants who appear before the court are 'guilty of something' and if they are acquitted, that they are 'lucky to get off', then it is also permissible to regard the courtroom experience itself as an exercise in deterrence, and to attempt to make it as unpleasant as possible for defendants.

Herbert Packer summarised the principles of the crime control model as follows:

> [it is] based on the proposition that the repression of criminal conduct by far the most important function to be performed by the criminal process . . . if the laws go unenforced — which is to say, if it is perceived that there is a high percentage of failure to apprehend and convict . . . the general disregard for legal controls tends to develop . . . In order to operate successfully the process must produce a high rate of apprehension and conviction . . . there must be a feeling of speed and finality . . .[6]

The whole of the criminal process from arrest to sentence should thus facilitate the processing of the offender in the interests of the ultimate objective of the system, that of controlling crime.

Rehabilitation and the Medical Model

This view of the social function of the criminal courts rejects concepts of guilt and punishment as meaningless. Rather it sees events that are called crimes simply as an occasion for social intervention. Far from being responsible for their actions, people are seen as the products and in some cases the victims of events beyond their control. Free will and moral responsibility are, according to this view, illusions. Rather than punishing people for committing crimes, therefore, society should find ways of meeting their needs by providing them with the requisite human social qualities for them to control their future behaviour and so convert them into law-abiding citizens.

According to the theory advances in the social sciences this century have already brought us closer to an understanding of the causes of crime and the court's role should therefore be to put this knowledge to practical use in the way in which it deals with offenders. The ideal objective for the criminal justice system should be neither deterrence nor the reduction of conflict but rehabilitation, that is the restoration of the defendant to a state of mental and social health whereby he will be able to cope with the demands society makes of him and refrain from conduct which might cause further intervention to be necessary.

The court process according to this perspective should resemble that of a clinic, where the successive objectives are diagnosis, prognosis, treatment and cure; hence the medical model. Ideally a court which operated according to the principles of this model would begin with the assumption that every person who appeared in the dock was in need of treatment and that the court was able through its expertise either to provide such treatment itself or refer the defendant to some other agency where the appropriate treatment would be available. It would then set about collecting information about the defendant's family background, his education, his medical history, his work record, his previous encounters with the criminal law, his present situation. All this information would be analysed by officials who through their expertise, qualifications and experience were skilled in diagnosing the causes of the defendant's anti-social behaviour, predicting the likelihood of further anti-social acts and proposing an appropriate course of treatment.

Defenders of the rehabilitative ideal, in response to criticisms that this 'soft' approach to criminals has failed to stem the crime wave and may rather encourage criminal conduct, are quick to point out that the criminal courts' application of the principles of rehabilitation has been only half-hearted. Moreover, they stress that the lack of adequate resources and manpower have further prevented any valid testing of the rehabilitation theory.[7] Furthermore, they argue, even if the attempts at treating rather than punishing defendants have not proved as effective as had been hoped, this is not in itself a sufficient argument for the abandonment of rehabilitation as an ideal for the courts, for the behavioural sciences are still in their infancy and as our knowledge increases so the skills of assessment, prediction and treatment will advance until ultimately something approaching perfection will be achieved. Until that time, the court should make use of such knowledge as is available rather than turning its back on the possibility of taking positive action to improve the defendant and making him better able to cope.

A further point concerning the application of the medical model is that sentences which the sentencers intend to have a rehabilitative objective may be perceived by defendants and others as punishment pure and simple or even may be seen as likely to impede rehabilitation. Thus, it is permissible for magistrates to send a defendant to prison or recommend him for borstal training and still remain within the precepts of the medical model, for, in theory at least, prison and borstal are places which are capable of dealing with the defendant's needs. Moreover, the mere fact that the treatment imposed by the court is unpleasant does not in itself deny its rehabilitative qualities for much medical treatment is unpleasant yet effective. Furthermore, unpleasantness may help to impress upon defendants the seriousness of their problems and the importance that their own efforts may play in overcoming these problems.

If the medical model provides an accurate explanation of the criminal justice process, one would clearly expect to find, first, procedures for collecting accurate and extensive information about the defendant, secondly, experience and expertise in diagnosis, prognosis and prediction and thirdly, a concern that the sentencers respond to the defendant's individual rehabilitative requirements. One would also expect the court proceedings to be conducted in an informal relaxed atmosphere where little attention would be paid to the strict rules of evidence or procedure, since these would obstruct attempts to uncover the defendant's problems and discuss ways to alleviate them.

Of the courtroom regulars, those most likely to subscribe to a rehabilitation approach are probation officers and social workers. In addition, the desire to help people less fortunate than themselves may be an important motivation not only for professional social workers, but also for some magistrates and lawyers and this motivation may find expression in their courtroom decisions and performances.

The Management of Crime and Criminals and the Bureaucratic Model

In every society there must be rules setting out what sorts of behaviour are not permitted and procedures for dealing with people who break these rules. The system which any particular society evolved for managing rule-breakers will depend upon the socio-economic ideology of that society. As regards our social system, 'both Marx and Weber, the two greatest students of capitalist development stressed the inseparable links between the origins of capitalism and the growth of formal political equality before the law as a legitimating principle of the liberal state'.[8] Since modern capitalism is based upon *calculation* and *rationality*

[I]t requires for its survival a system of justice whose workings can be rationally calculated, at least in principle, according to fixed general terms, just as the probable performance of a machine can be calculated . . .[9]

For Weber, as Balbus remarks, 'the spirit of capitalism and the spirit of formal legal rationality were two sides of the same coin'.[10] The demands of the liberal capitalist state 'required that the legal system be insulated from the immediate political conflicts of the day' and embodied 'a framework of substantive and procedural norms binding upon and serviceable to both the government and the governed'.[11] Applied to the criminal justice system, this meant that the courts must be seen as 'neutral before the conflict between state and the accused'.[12] Each defendant, no matter what his race, colour, creed, social status or political beliefs may be, must be seen as submitting to the same rational assessment of his conduct in accordance with predetermined formal rules of procedure and evidence which 'subordinate political and other discretion . . . and arbitrary and irrational decisions'.[13]

There is then clearly a close relationship between due process ideals and the bureaucratic model. However, whereas the primary concern of due process is the protection of the individual against the arbitrary power of the state, the bureaucratic objective is to process defendants according to standard procedures, a closed system of rules which operate independently of political considerations and regardless of who is in the dock. This bureaucratic approach is likely to be adopted to a greater or lesser degree by the clerk to the justices and the other court clerks at the magistrates' court.[14]

Any system charged with the management of conflicting interests and decision-making and the distribution of resources must apply the operational principles which the bureaucratic model brings to the fore. As Max Weber points out, bureaucratic institutions in general place a heavy emphasis upon 'precision, speech consistency, the availability of records, continuity and the minimization of friction and of expense for materials and personnel'.[15] Applying these concepts to the criminal justice system as it affects guilty pleaders in magistrates' courts one would expect to find encouragement and rewards given to any procedures, strategies and decisions which saved time and expedited the processing of cases; conversely, one would expect to see discouragements and sanctions applied to time-wasting and the prolongation of cases. Since tensions and hostility between participants is unpredictable and thus potentially disruptive, and the nature of the criminal courts' business is such as to generate high levels of emotion, one would also expect to find devices for reducing conflict to the minimum and ways of stifling any threats to the smoothness of the proceedings.

Another essential aspect of any bureaucracy that one would expect to find in a court operating according to a bureaucratic model is the important status given to records. Records are vital to the efficiency of any bureaucracy in a number of ways. They contain readily accessible information on all past transactions. Without such information the administration would have to rely upon the fallible memories of participants. They permit the accumulation in one place of information from several different sources. A defendant's 'file' may, for example, contain a record of his prior convictions, a social enquiry report, a psychiatric report and a record of his previous court appearances on the present charge. Finally, in accepting the record as the only reliable account of past events and the only reliable source of information, much time and labour may be saved, for a strong presumption may exist that anything appearing in the record is not open to question and that anything that does not appear in the record is irrelevant, unreliable or otherwise unacceptable as evidence. Such a presumption may add considerably to the fulfilment of the bureaucratic objectives of speed and efficiency.

The economic use of resources is also an important feature of the bureaucratic model that one would expect to find in the functioning of police forces, lawyers' offices and the magistrates' courts, according to this model. Resources in this context may refer simply to material considerations. The court may operate on a limited budget and must distribute its resources in the most cost-effective manner. It may also refer to the various court professionals, the representatives of different agencies and interests who use the magistrates' court to conduct their business: or policemen, probation officers, magistrates, court clerks, lawyers. All of these groups are of course subject to a greater or lesser degree to bureaucratic demands and constraints arising from the particular organisation or business to which they belong. A bureaucratic perspective would see all contributing in different ways, with little or no duplication, to the efficient running of the magistrates' courts. This presupposes some clear delineation of their roles and a division of labour which takes into account their respective skills, resources and limitations.

Status Degradation, Denunciation and the Status Passage Model

This perspective stresses the function of the criminal courts as institutions for denouncing the defendant, reducing his social status and so promoting solidarity within the community. The reduction of social status in the offender results, according to this theoretical perspective, not only in the stigmatisation of the defendant as a person with a tarnished moral character, but also in the enhancement of social cohesiveness among law-abiding members of the community by setting the defendant apart from the community and by emphasising the difference between him and law-abiding citizens.

A person's status is the position he has reached as a member of society and reflects his self-image as well as the opinions of others as to his social value. The length of time a person holds a particular status may vary considerably, but each status is of limited duration.

> Status passage occurs whenever there is a movement on the part of the individual to a different part of the social structure involving a loss or gain of privilege or power and a changed identity and sense of self. The concept of status passage covers a wide variety of situations from illness to job promotion, from marriage to dying.[16]

In our society a person's status is closely related to his moral standing in the community. With a few notable exceptions such as pop stars, actors, writers and artists, those people who are found to be in breach of the accepted moral code by, for example, committing acts of dishonesty, taking prohibited drugs or engaging in deviant sexual activities are likely to experience a lowering of status. While law and morality are clearly not identical, and breaking the criminal law is not necessarily the same as contravening the moral code, there is nevertheless a sufficient concordance between the two concepts for the criminal courts to be regarded as places where the moral standing of citizens is put in issue. In many cases then the social function of the court may be seen as that of moral condemnation and hence degradation of status. Whenever the court condemns, denounces and 'degrades' the defendant, it reaffirms the moral values of the community and by doing so, strengthens community solidarity.[17]

Unlike the other process models discussed in this chapter, status passage places particular emphasis on the ritual aspects of magistrates' courts. The courtroom ceremony, according to this model, is not just performance devoid of any meaning or purpose, designed merely to distract the public's attention from the important business of the criminal justice system which is carried on 'behind the scenes'. Rather, the ceremony, or at least the one where the defendant pleads guilty and is sentenced, marks the culmination of the process of denunciation and degradation. The preceding steps in the process are seen as a preparation for this moment. One would expect, therefore, that a court process that conformed to this model would reserve for the public ceremony its attempts to denounce the defendant, to shame him and reduce his status in the eyes of the community.

Garfinkel suggests that in all societies that are not 'completely demoralized' status degradation ceremonies exist and that their function is to transform the public identity 'into something looked on as lower in the local scheme of social types'.[18] Degradation ceremonies, according to Garfinkel, have two paradigms — a behavioural paradigm and a moral indignation paradigm. The behavioural paradigm is that of shame and guilt and may be

> found in the phrases that denote removal of the self from the public view, i.e. removal from the regard of the publicly identified other: 'I could have sunk through the floor; I wanted to run away and hide; I wanted the earth to open up and swallow me.'[19]

and 'in the behaviour of self-abnegation — disgust, the rejection of further contact with or withdrawal from . . .'[20]

The other paradigm, that of moral indignation, is, according to Garfinkel, *public* denunciation. 'We publicly deliver the curse: I call upon all men to bear witness that he is not as he appears to be but is otherwise and *in essence* of a lower species.'[21]

Just as there are two aspects to deterrence, therefore, there are two distinct paradigms implicit in denunciation, one private, relating to the individual's reaction, and the other public, relating to the effect of the denunciation upon the community. Thus Garfinkel comments that 'Moral indignation serves to effect the ritual destruction of the person denounced. Unlike shame, which does not bind persons together, moral indignation may reinforce group solidarity.'[22]

Garfinkel goes on to identify those features of a degradation ceremony which make for successful denunciation. They include the fixing of distance between the person being denounced and the denouncer and witness, the ritual separation of the denounced person from a place in the legitimate order ('i.e. he must be defined as standing at a place opposed to it'[23] and the removal of both the event and the perpetrator from the realm of their everyday character so that they stand as 'out of the ordinary'.

Since social status is a function of community values and community response, for effective degradation there would have to exist efficient methods of transmitting details of the degradation ceremony to the community. Moreover, as status degraders and moral denouncers the magistrates would have to be perceived by the defendant and by the public as representing the values of the community. This continuous two-way exchange between the court and the community would then be an essential feature of a magistrates' court process based upon the status passage model.

Another important feature that one would expect to find is the existence of 'passage agents'. Perhaps the most obvious example of passage agents are the doctors, surgeons and nurses who are responsible for the passage of hospital patients. These agents interpret, define and legitimate the passage. They serve the person undergoing the passage (the passagee) as expert guide and sign readers, able to predict what course the passage will take and having the ability to a lesser or greater degree to alter that course. Where it is in the interests of passage agents that the passage should take a specific course they will attempt to control the passage, and deny control to the passagee and other agents. Where total control is not feasible, they will through strategy and negotiation attempt to seize for themselves as much control as possible.[24]

The Maintenance of Class Domination and the Power Model

This approach to the criminal justice system sees the system as promoting the interests of a ruling class and maintaining its position of dominance over other groups in society. For our purposes it is not important to identify the various shades of political ideology associated with the basic concept that the courts together with other social institutions form part of the apparatus of the state which helps to maintain and reproduce class dominance. Nor is it necessary for us to differentiate between the ways in which different radical critics of the legal system have interpreted its operation in relation to the notion of class dominance. To some extent it is inevitable that what is presented here is something of a caricature of these various theoretical approaches, for to be otherwise would involve a lengthy and detailed examination of the writings of a large number of authors, an exercise which is beyond the limited scope of this study. Furthermore, it is not important for us to identify with any precision the particular groups involved as dominating or being dominated. Suffice it to mention that the view of the criminal justice system as unjust, discriminatory and oppressive towards certain groups in our society has been used to describe the operation of the system towards the working class in general and, more specifically, towards specific sections such as the blacks or, in Northern Ireland, the Roman Catholics.[25]

In the previous discussion on the nature of the law in a liberal, capitalist state, it was stated that capitalism and formal legal rationality were, according to Weber, 'two sides of the same coin'. However, where the substantive goal of the power elite or dominant group within society is repression and the maintenance of the existing social order at any cost, a conflict is bound to occur between the efforts to achieve these goals and the substantive rationality of the legal system. In other words, close adherence in practice to the liberal principles which characterise due process rules and the humane treatment of defendants is likely to obstruct rather than assist the dominant class in maintaining social control. In these circumstances, there will be tension between formal rationality and substantive rationality, between the letter and the practice of the law; 'The effort to maintain "law *and* order" thus tends to degenerate into a choice between law *or* order.'[26] Yet by choosing 'order' — social control by whatever repressive means are at its disposal — the dominant class in a liberal state risks losing consensus support, which might in turn lead to popular dissaffection and the eventual overthrow of the existing order. One solution to this dilemma available to the power elite is to present a facade of formal legal rationality while permitting coercive and irrational methods of control to operate up to a point behind this facade.[27] Another possibility is to allow flexibility and discretion in the interpretation of the formal rules, so that, although on the face of things, these rules appear to offer assurances of fair play and equal treatment for all members of society and rational, considered decision-making, in fact they give considerable scope for discrimination and repression.

Unlike the bureaucratic approach which assumes the independence of the criminal justice system from the state and its neutrality in the conflicts that arise between state and individual, this perspective sees the courts and the agents of criminal justice very much as part of the state machinery, a machinery which is dominated by the interests of the ruling class. This does not mean that policemen, lawyers, magistrates, clerks and probation officers are all conspirators in a plot to maintain and perpetuate the dominance of the ruling class, but rather that the state creates the conditions by which through the pursuit of their apparent self-interests each of these groups helps to advance the interests of the state and thus the dominant power elite. For example, policemen may be more concerned with their arrest and conviction records than with abstract ideals of justice and integrity. This may lead to the use of oppressive measures to ensure high conviction rates, which, in turn, may enhance the interests of the state.

To attempt to construct a process model applicable to guilty plead-ers in magistrates' courts out of this perspective is clearly problematic, for one is faced with the paradox that the power elite, in order to dominate by consent rather than by the naked use of force, must give the impression of formal legal rationality. Yet one feature one might expect to find is the existence of glaring contradictions between the official versions of the system's operation and what happens in practice. One would anticipate that the official version would emphasise the due process and humanitarian values of the system together with the competence of the decision-makers to make rational, objective choices. The practical operation of the system, on the other hand, would be likely to involve obvious elements of coercion and discrimination as well as decisions based on class values operating to the detriment of the oppressed classes. These features would naturally be denied by those wishing to uphold the official version or at least explained away in terms which excluded the possibility of systematic class oppression. Finally, one would expect the operation of the system to be in the hands of people who, while differing in their roles within and the objectives they seek from criminal justice, nevertheless share the same basic assumptions concerning the system's aims, its place within the larger social arena and the stance it should adopt towards crime and criminals. Since these assumptions will have been generated by and reinforced according to a class-bound view of society and the nature of law, one would anticipate that outsiders to that class will view it with a sense of absurdity and disbelief.[28]

5. The Relationship between the Process Models

The six process models are, as we have seen, related to six very different ideological approaches to the criminal justice system and to six very distinct objectives that may be attributed to magistrates' courts or, for that matter, to any criminal court. However, the models clearly owe their origins to dissimilar sources and it would be a mistake to proceed any further with this analysis without spelling out these distinctions and without placing the models in some sort of theoretical context.

Three of the models — due process, crime control and medical — could be described as 'participant approaches' in that to a greater or lesser degree they reflect the values and perspectives of one or more of the groups of regular participants in the magistrates' court. A criminal justice system, for example, which put into effect those features associated with the crime control model would be likely to find favour with the majority of policemen and, I suspect, many magistrates. Similarly, most probation officers would probably approve of those features associated with the medical model and most defence lawyers with the promotion of due process ideals. This does not, of course, mean to say that every last policeman and each and every probation officer or defence lawyer will automatically subscribe to every feature of the model associated with their participant group to the exclusion of everything else. Some policemen, for instance, may well believe in the rights of the citizen to protection from the state or in the need to help rather than punish some types of offenders. Likewise some probation officers might appreciate the need for formal procedures in court proceedings or acknowledge the importance of the court's deterrent role, even if these aspects of magistrates' court proceedings make their own task more difficult.

Moreover, some participants may not favour in any general way any one of these three 'participant' models. Rather, they may apply them selectively depending on their perception of the type of case or the type of defendant they are dealing with. The models then are 'ideal types' in Weber's sense of the term. While they do not claim to represent the attitudes of individual actors, they are each distillations of a perspective, an approach to criminal justice which one would expect to prevail among particular groups of participants. This does not mean to say that the perspectives are exclusive to those who take a regular role in the criminal courts. Indeed, as we shall see in the final chapter, they are present among politicians, civil servants, media men and in the general population, for it is these models that provide the conceptual framework for the public debate on contemporary society's response to crime and criminals. Each of the three models in its own way offers answers to questions about current social policy. They provide the policy-makers and the public with a ready-made stance to take towards problems thrown up by the criminal justice system such as the remand in custody of defendants who are subsequently acquitted, inconsistencies in sentencing or the rejection of suspect confessions.

The other three models, however, are very different both in their origins and in the sorts of questions to which they may provide answers. These models are analytical and theoretical; they are derived from the work of social theorists who seek to explain the structure of society, the interrelationships between social institutions within that structure and the forces which bring about social change or which resist attempts at change. They do not attempt to describe the attitudes of the regular participants nor identify the conscious motives for their behaviour. They do not provide the magistrates' courts with a blueprint for reform or suggest that reforms should take any particular direction. The bureaucratic model, for example, does not commend the bureaucratic nature of contemporary social institutions, nor does it offer any criticism as such. Rather, it presents bureaucratisation and the pursuit of bureaucratic objectives as inevitable for complex organisations within an advanced capitalist society. Similarly, status passage theory does not *propose* that the courts be used to denounce and degrade people, but suggests that courts, in common with several other institutions, share this important social function. The same could be said about the 'power model' in that it does not prescribe class domination as a laudable social objective, but rather sees such domination as characterising the operation of institutions within capitalist societies and the relationships between individuals within those institutions.

Although some of the proponents of these three 'social models' might argue that each one provides a total view of the magistrates' court process, that taken on its own, it will give a complete explanation for everything that takes place in magistrates' courts, for the purposes of this study it is suggested that the picture offered by each individual model is only a partial one and that the full picture (or as close as one is likely to come to a full picture) will emerge only after applying several different models, viewing the system from several different perspectives. In terms of the perspectives they offer, the 'social models' differ from the 'participant models' in the fact that they emphasise the contributions of all the participants towards the fulfilment of some overriding social objective rather than drawing attention to the specific roles of particular groups of participants and the conflict that emerge as each group struggles to attain its particular goals. According to the 'social models', therefore, all the courtroom regulars, police, lawyers, clerks, magistrates and probation officers, are engaged in one social process, be it the management of crime, the reduction of social status or the maintenance of power in the hands of the class elite.

What then are the differences between the strategic approaches that these two sets of models propose towards the analysis of empirical information concerning magistrates' courts which we shall be undertaking in subsequent chapters? In the first place, the 'participant mod-

els' propose clear ideals for the attainment of due process, crime
control and rehabilitation objectives. By measuring these ideals against
the formal and informal knowledge concerning the operation of the
magistrates' courts process it should be possible to evaluate the extent
to which the system succeeds or fails in achieving these ideals, to identify, in other words, the gap between aspiration and performance. The
social models should complement this analysis by offering explanations,
first, as to why the system should pursue certain policy goals or give
the impression that it is pursuing these goals and, secondly, as to why
gaps might occur between aspiration and performance or contradictions emerge from the court's attempts to achieve multiple objectives.
The 'social models', unlike their 'participant' counterparts, may also
be able to throw new light upon the routine, taken-for-granted procedures of the court and role-playing of the participants. They may raise
questions which are rarely, if ever, considered, highlight aspects of
the system which tend to be ignored and provide new and stimulating
interpretations of the routine and the familiar.

Notes

1. See e.g. S. Bedford, *The Faces of Justice* (Collins, London, 1961).

2. H. Packer, *The Limits of the Criminal Sanction* (Stanford University Press, 1969).

3. Packer, *ibid.*, pp. 163 and 165.

4. Ibid., p. 159.

5. Ibid., pp. 160-1.

6. Ibid., pp. 158-9.

7. See e.g. editorial, *New Law Journal* (10 May 1979), pp. 454-5.

8. I. Balbus, *The Dialectics of Legal Repression* (Russell Sage Foundation, New York, 1973), p.4.

9. G. Lukács, *History and Class Consciousness* (Merlin Press, London, 1971), p. 96.

10. Balbus, *Dialectics*, p. 4.

11. Ibid., p. 5.

12. Ibid., p. 10.

13. Ibid., p. 13.

14. A. E. Bottoms and J. D. McClean, *Defendants in the Criminal Process* (Routledge and Kegan Paul, London, 1976), p. 228.

15. M. Rheinstein (ed.), *Max Weber on Law in Economy and Society* (Harvard University Press, Cambridge, Mass, 1954), extract cited in L. Friedman and S. Macauley (ed). *Law and the Behavioural Sciences*, 2nd edn (Bobbs-Merrill, Indianapolis: New York, 1977), p. 989.

16. M. King, 'A Status Passage Analysis of the Defendant's Progress through the Magistrates' Court', *Law and Human Behaviour*, vol. 2, no. 3 (1978), p. 187. See also B. Glazer and A. Strauss, *Status Passage* (Routledge and Kegan Paul, London, 1971).

17. See E. Durkheim, *The Division of Labour in Society*, translated by G. Simpson (Macmillan, London, 1933), pp. 108-9.

18. H. Garfinkel, 'Conditions of Successful Degradation Ceremonies', *American Journal of Sociology*, vol. 6 (1956), pp. 420–4.

19. Ibid.

20. Ibid.

21. Ibid.

22. Ibid.

23. Ibid.

24. See B. Glazer and A. Strauss, *Status Passage*, pp. 5 and 58.

25. See Balbus, *Dialectics;* S. Hall *et al.*, *Policing the Crisis: Muggings, The State and Law and Order* (Macmillan, London, 1978); T. Hadden and P. Hillyard, *Justice in Northern Ireland* (Cobden Trust, London, 1973).

26. Balbus, *Dialectics*, p. 11.

27. See P. Carlen *Magistrates' Justice* (Martin Robertson, London, 1976).

28. See Carlen, *Magistrates' Justice* and Z. Bankowski and G. Mungham, *Images of Law* (Routledge and Kegan Paul, London, 1976).

3
The Formal Process

1. Who are the Guilty Pleaders?

Every year roughly 40 in every 1,000 people become defendants in magistrates' courts. Some, the minor motoring offenders, never appear in the courtroom, but even if one ignores all motoring cases, in 1977 this would still have left just under 943,000 people or approximately 18 in every 1,000 adult citizens of England and Wales, who will have faced the magistrates, charged with breaking the criminal law.[1] Since the last century criminologists have sought factors which distinguish 'criminals' from law-abiding citizens, but with a singular lack of success. Some offenders may be physically or psychologically abnormal, but the only characteristic that differentiates the vast majority from the ordinary citizen is the fact that they have been convicted of a crime. In other words, they have broken the criminal law and attracted the attention of the authorities, who have decided to prosecute.

What we do know about those who are prosecuted is that the overwhelming majority are young males. In 1977 male defendants outnumbered female by a proportion of over six to one, despite the fact that the number of female offenders has been rising dramatically over recent years. The official statistics also indicate that the chances of prosecution and conviction for indictable (more serious) offences decrease substantially as people get older. For example, the rate of convictions for the 21-24 age group in 1977 was 3,600 in every 100,000 compared to 1,547 for the 30-40 age group.[2] These statistics contain no information about the social backgrounds of offenders. However, both general knowledge and recent surveys that have been carried out in the criminal courts point to the conclusion that they come predominantly from the Registrar General's social classes III, IV and V, that is, from the ranks of the clerical and manual workers.[3] Since the overwhelming majority of defendants plead guilty irrespective of their age, sex or class background, we can safely conclude that the average guilty pleader in the magistrates' court is likely to be male, under 25 and from one of the lower income groups. As a conclusion, however, this is none too helpful, for it does not depart from the stereotype we all have of defendants in criminal courts. Nor does it give any indication that many guilty pleaders bear no resemblance to this statistical average, as anyone who sits through a morning at a busy court will discover. Moreover, the stereotype tends to conceal differences between defendants which have nothing to do with age, sex or social class. Personality differences between defendants may, for example, mean that they respond in very different ways to the experience of being brought before the court. The extent of their knowledge and previous experience of the criminal justice process may also affect in different ways their reactions and their decisions when confronted with the possibility of a criminal conviction and punishment at the hands of the magistrates. In discussing guilty pleaders, defendants or suspects it is very difficult to avoid having some stereotype image in the back of one's mind. In writing this book, moreover, it has been impossible to avoid using words which conjure up these stereotypes and equally impossible to make fine distinctions between different types of defendants each time these words occur. The reader must, therefore, to some extent be his own control and try to avoid picturing either the police stereotype of the hardened professional or the liberal 'do-gooder's' image of the helpless, inadequate victim of society or, for that matter, the statistically average male, working-class youth and concentrate not so much on the characteristics of the defendants as on the common situations in which they find themselves.

2. Police Powers and Duties

One way of considering the formal rules which govern the criminal justice process is to identify the powers, duties and limitations on those powers which the law provides in respect of each of the participants to the process and which may affect the behaviour of those and the other participants. This is not to imply that the rules are always obeyed to the letter or that sanctions are always imposed whenever the rules are broken. As we shall see in subsequent discussions, this is far from the case. All we are concerned with here, however, are those legal formalities which provide a framework for the actions of the participants to the magistrates' courts.

One can divide police powers roughly into three categories. First, there are powers relating to the obtaining of evidence, secondly, powers relating to the detention of people suspected or accused of crimes and thirdly, the power to prosecute. In practice, the first two sets of powers may in many cases complement one another. The first category covers the search of suspects and their premises and the seizure of items which might be relevant as evidence in a subsequent criminal trial. Generally, the police may not stop and search people, but a number of statutes give them specific powers to search for particular items where they have 'reason to suspect' or 'reasonable grounds for suspecting' that the person stopped has such items on him. These include drugs,[4] firearms,[5] stolen goods[6] and bird eggs.[7] Most of these statutes also give the police power to search any vehicle in which the suspect is travelling. For the purposes of our analysis these powers are important in that they may account, particularly in inner city areas, for a substantial proportion of arrests and subsequent convictions. One author of a study of the Metropolitan Police claimed that 'stops' constituted 40 per cent of arrests each year.[8]

Having taken a person to the police station and having decided to charge him or her with a criminal offence, it is common practice for the police to require fingerprints and photographs. There is no legal authority requiring defendants to submit to these procedures, but in the case of fingerprinting, if they refuse, the police may apply to the magistrates for an order.[9] So far as photographs are concerned, however, the only situation in which they may insist that a person have photographs taken is where he or she has been arrested under the Prevention of Terrorism (Temporary Provisions) Act 1976. It is becoming increasingly common for the police to require people to submit to medical examinations at the police station. Once again, they have no statutory powers to make such examinations compulsory, except in mental health[10] and immigration cases.[11] However, failure to provide a specimen of blood or urine without reasonable excuse will render a person arrested on suspicion of driving with excess alcohol guilty of an offence under the Road Traffic Act 1972.

Turning now to the policeman's powers in relation to verbal evidence, there is absolutely no obligation for people stopped by the police to answer questions even to identify themselves except for a car driver where a traffic offence is alleged.[12] Even when the police take someone to the police station for questioning, there is nothing in law to compel him or her to answer questions. They may, of course, encourage a suspect to talk, but the temptation to go further than mere encouragement is inhibited, at least in theory, by the risk that any confession that the suspect may make may be rejected by the court on the grounds that it was not made voluntarily. This fundamental principle of law is summarised in the introduction to the Judges' Rules, which states that

> it is a fundamental condition of the admissibility in evidence of any oral answer given by that person to a question put by a police officer and of any statement made by that person, that it shall have been voluntary, in the sense that it has not been obtained from him by fear of prejudice or hope of advantage, exercised or held out by a person in authority, or by oppression. (*R. v. Prager*)

The term 'oppression' has been defined in the courts as meaning

> something which tends to sap and has sapped that free will which must exist before a confession is voluntary . . . Whether or not there is oppression in an individual case depends upon many elements . . . They include such things as the length of time of any individual periods of questioning, the length of time intervening between periods of questioning, whether the accused person has been given proper refreshment or not, and the characteristics of the person who makes the statement.[13]

Where disputes take place, therefore, between prosecution and defence as to whether the defendant's statement to the police was made voluntarily, the court first has to decide whose account of events to believe, for rarely is there agreement between the police and defendants. It then has to determine whether the threats, inducement or oppression were such as to make it unsafe for the confession to be accepted as evidence. In the magistrates' court, where, of course, there is no jury, these decisions are the responsibility of the bench of magistrates which then goes on to decide whether or not the defendant is guilty. In other words unlike a jury, they may in their consideration of the evidence be aware of the contents of a a confession statement which they had previously decided was inadmissible.[14] This strange situation and the fact that both judges and magistrates have a wide discretion in deciding who to believe and what evidence to reject as unsafe, according to many commentators, tends to reduce any impact these rules might have had on police conduct, had they been strictly interpreted and applied, as in the United States, where any evidence which the police have obtained by breaking the rules is automatically excluded and, even where the case is tried without a jury, there is a preliminary hearing before a different judge to the trial judge to decide what evidence is admissible.[15] Such statistics as are available would appear to indicate that the police in this country have little difficulty in obtaining confessions from suspects, despite the legal constraints on their conduct. One study carried out at Sheffield indicated that as many as 70 per cent of defendants confessed straight away while a further 24 per cent admitted their guilt later on.[16]

There are detailed restrictions on police conduct and specific directions for the treatment and interrogation of suspects contained in the Judges' Rules.[17] These cover such matters as cautioning the suspect before questioning — 'You are not obliged to say anything unless you wish to do so but what you say may be put into writing and given in evidence' — providing him with refreshment, taking down the suspect's own words, asking him to read the statement before he signs it. It is important to note, however, that these rules do not carry the weight of law. They are administrative directions and their breach, while possibly giving rise to disciplinary proceedings against the police officers concerned, does not in itself affect the validity of the confession, unless the judge or magistrates decide that the breach is sufficiently important for the evidence to be excluded. The provision which has attracted the most attention from courts and researchers is that contained in the Preamble to the Rules which states that the Judges' Rules do not affect the principle that

> every person at any state of an investigation should be able to communicate and to consult privately with a solicitor. This is so even if he is in custody provided that in such a case no unreasonable delay or hindrance is caused to the processes of investigation or the administration of justice by his doing so.[18]

Two independent research studies have indicated that a substantial proportion — some 75 per cent — of those defendants who had asked to see a solicitor were not permitted to do so.[19] Yet only very rarely has a judge exercised his discretion to exclude evidence made by the accused after the police had refused to allow him to contact a solicitor. One judge did so in order that 'it may do something to put an end to an undesirable practice' on the part of the police.[20] In several other recent cases the judge has exercised his discretion in the opposite direction,[21] and the general rule appears to be that expressed in *Prager* and mentioned earlier, that it all depends on whether the judge is satisfied that the statement was made voluntarily.[22] Once again, it would appear that the formal law has very little effect upon the behaviour of the police. A recent change in the law, which now requires the police to inform a person named by the suspect that he, the suspect, has been arrested and is being held in custody[23] in a police station, is unlikely to alter this situation, since, in the first place, it applies only to those suspects who have been formally arrested,[24] and, secondly, it allows the police to delay giving this information, 'where some delay is necessary in the interest of the investigation or prevention of crime or the apprehension of offenders . . . '

Turning to the second category of police powers, the powers of arrest and detention, a police officer who has reasonable suspicion that a person has committed, is committing or is about to commit an 'arrestable offence' may arrest that person.[25] He must tell the person that he or she is being arrested[26] and the reason for the arrest.[27] Failure to do so makes the arrest unlawful and could result in an action in the civil court for damages against the police officer concerned or in disciplinary proceedings, although it must be added that civil actions are extremely rare and complaints against the police of wrongful arrest or failure to give information on arrest are almost as infrequent. One reason is the wide discretion given to individual police officers by the words 'reasonable suspicion'. Another reason is the fact that in many cases the police officer will not formally arrest a suspect, but will merely ask him or her to 'come along to the police station to answer some questions'. Only if the suspect resists or refuses to accompany the officer is a formal arrest likely to take place.

The police may also apply to a single magistrate for an arrest warrant where the offence is indictable or punishable with imprisonment or where the defendant's address is not sufficiently established for a summons to be served on him.[28] The magistrate who issues the warrant has a discretion whether or not to endorse it for bail. If he does so, then the police must release the defendant once they have arrested, interrogated and charged him or her. If the warrant is not endorsed for bail, then the police must bring the defendant before the magistrates at the earliest opportunity after charging him or her and may hold him or her in custody until then.

A person who has not been arrested but is being held by the police for questioning cannot, according to basic legal principles, be compelled to remain at the police station against his or her will.[29] Any attempt to leave the police station, however, will probably be met with a formal arrest. Once a person has been 'taken into custody for an offence without a warrant' he or she must be brought before the magistrates as soon as practicable[30] and where it is not practicable to do so within 24 hours, the police must release him or her on bail, unless it appears to the police to be a 'serious case'.[31] Neither 'taken into custody' nor 'serious case' are defined by the Act or subsequent case law, although the police interpretation is that the provisions apply only after a person has been charged, when the 'reasonable suspicion' they held when they arrested or detained the defendant has become 'prima facie evidence' for a charge to be brought.[32] This means that, according to the police, they may hold a person for periods exceeding 24 hours without bringing that person before the magistrates' court, providing that they do not charge him or her. As we shall see, the 'greyness' or lack of certainty that surrounds police powers between arrest or detention and being charged may have an important influence on the conduct of policemen and suspects.

The only legal remedy open to a person being held by the police is to issue a writ of habeas corpus. However, this remedy is largely illusory for a number of reasons.[33] First, it depends on someone else knowing of the detention and being willing to take action in the court. Although Section 62 of the Criminal Law Act 1977 does oblige the police to inform a person reasonably named by the defendant that he has been arrested, the police may hold someone without formally arresting him and, moreover, are entitled to delay disclosure 'in the interest of the investigation or prevention of crime or the apprehension of offenders'. This section and its implications are discussed in detail in Chapter 6. Secondly, procedural complications and the fact that the application must normally be made to the Divisional Court of the Queen's Bench in London often result in delays, particularly for an applicant outside London. Thirdly, even when the case finally reaches the court, the practice appears to have developed to adjourn it to allow the police to be represented and to present their case. It may, therefore, take two or three days before a hearing actually takes place and even longer if a weekend intervenes. By this time the police will probably have released their prisoner or brought him or her before the magistrates.

It should not, however, be imagined that the police in almost every case detain the defendant in police stations for a long period. The official statistics, while giving no indication as to how long defendants were held before being charged do show that in 1977 25 per cent of defendants were summonsed and, therefore, were not subject to police discretion as to bail or custody before their magistrates' court appearance, while 60 per cent were released on bail having been charged.

Only 15 per cent were actually refused bail by the police. But one must emphasise that a proportion of those released on bail and even some of those who were eventually summonsed may have spent time at the police station under interrogation or locked up in the cells.

3. The Magistrates

In 1975 there were 680 adult magistrates' courts in in England and Wales involving about 20,000 magistrates and providing approximately a quarter of a million court sittings every year. Five hundred of these courts are situated in rural areas or small towns, while the remaining 180 are located in conurbations and large towns. They deal not only with criminal cases, but also with licensing applications for sales of alcohol and for betting shops, with matrimonial cases, with applications for affiliation orders and adoption and, as juvenile courts, with a wide range of cases involving the welfare of children. Many of the criminal cases dealt with by magistrates are trivial in nature, consisting of minor motoring offences or fiscal offences such as the non-payment of motor tax or TV licence fee. In fact, of all the 2,100,000 defendants processed by magistrates in 1977, 55 per cent were charged with less serious motoring offences, such as speeding and driving without due care. Yet even for the more serious criminal cases the overwhelming majority of defendants do not contest the case against them. In 1977, of all the 477,900 adults and juveniles who were charged with indictable or summary offences 85 per cent pleaded guilty to all charges in the magistrates' court.

There are two varieties of magistrates, stipendiaries, who are full-time professionals chosen from barristers and solicitors of at least seven years' standing[34] and law magistrates who, as their name suggests, are unpaid members of the public with no professional training in law. All magistrates are appointed by the Lord Chancellor,[35] the lay magistrates from a list of names recommended to him by a number of advisory committees which sit in secret in each administrative area. Not only are the sessions of these committees secret, but also the identity of the members. This system of appointing lay magistrates was first established in 1910 and has remained virtually unchanged since then.[36] Studies of the sort of people who become magistrates have revealed that they are more likely to be a member of a political party than the average member of the community and the political party they are most likely to belong to is Conservative.[37] One survey of magistrates appointed between 1971 and 1972 showed that weekly wage-earners made up only 13 per cent of male appointees. Of these unskilled or semi-skilled workers accounted for less than 1 per cent of the total male appointees. This contrasts with an intake from the professional and managerial classes of around 27 per cent.[38] It is clear, therefore, that in terms of employment and political affiliation the lay magistracy is hardly representative of the community as a whole. Even on a local basis there are some surprising anomalies. A parliamentary question in 1977 revealed, for example, that Tamworth, an industrial area, had a bench which consisted of only two wage-earners.[39] Another example is a detailed analysis of the bench at Rochdale in Lancashire which revealed that 49 per cent of the magistrates were members of the Rotary Club or its women's equivalent and at least 28 per cent were freemasons.[40] In terms of age and sex, however, the magistrates are rather more representative of the community, while coming nowhere near to reflecting the actual distribution of ages and genders in the population. A survey carried out in 1967 showed that women made up 30 per cent of lay justices and the average age of all lay magistrates was 56.[41] The 1972 study of recent appointees indicated both the proportion of women was increasing and the average age coming down.[42]

Compulsory training for magistrates was introduced in 1966 and is based on the recommendations set out in the 1965 White Paper, *The Training of Justices*. This provides for a two stage training scheme. Stage I training is supposed to take place before a magistrate starts adjudicating on the bench and to consist of elementary instruction on the role of the magistracy, evidence, court procedure and ways of dealing with offenders coupled with periods of court observation. Stage II, which must normally be completed within a year of appointment, consists of more detailed instruction, and visits to penal institutions. In a survey carried out by John Baldwin[43] in 1974, it was found that the recommendations of the White Paper were a long way from being implemented in many courts. A substantial proportion of new magistrates had begun adjudicating without having completed Stage I, observed court on at least three occasions or visited penal institutions. Baldwin's survey also revealed that for 11.4 per cent of magistrates the only lectures they received during their training programme came from a justices' clerk.

4. The Court Clerks

Whenever magistrates, whether lay or stipendiary, sit in court they must have a court clerk to assist them. Although the clerk is not himself a judicial decision-maker, he plays an important part in court proceedings, particularly in lay magistrates' courts, as the magistrates often refer to him on points of law or procedure and in practice leave much of the running of the court to him. Section 5(3) of the Justice of the Peace Act 1968 provides that among the duties of the clerk are (a) giving magistrates advice on law and procedure when they request it, and (b) bringing the magistrates' attention to any such matters. The magistrates must not seek the clerk's views on issues of facts and it is improper for them to listen to his views on these issues or even to request him to retire with them when no points of law on which they need advice arise in the case.[44]

Responsibility for the general administration of each magistrates' court is in the hands of the Clerk to the Justices, a sort of chief clerk. He is aided by assistant clerks, whose numbers depend on the size of the court and the extent of its business. Both the Clerk to the Justices and the assistants sit in court as court clerks. Although an increasing proportion of court clerks are qualified either as solicitors or barristers, there are still a large number who have no formal legal qualifications. According to the Home Office, even 20 per cent of the Clerks to the Justices were 'qualified by experience'.[45] Even today, few courts require all their clerks to be qualified and one court is known to operate about ten simultaneous courtrooms with only one qualified clerk in the building.

5. The Pre-sentencing Powers of Magistrates' Courts

The two major issues which arise by the time defendants in criminal cases make their first appearance in court are those of bail and legal aid. Should the defendant be released before his trial and should the state pay for or contribute towards the cost of a lawyer to advise and represent him or her? The first of these issues takes up a considerable amount of court time, since these days, in all but the most simple and straightforward of cases, such as a guilty plea to drunk and disorderly, it is usual for matters to be adjourned at the first hearing to enable the defendant to obtain legal advice or to give the defence or prosecution time to prepare its case. The Bail Act 1976 sets out the legal rules and principles which govern the granting and refusal of bail. It states that defendants charged with imprisonable offences should be granted bail unless there are 'substantial grounds for believing' that if released a defendant would:

    (a) fail to surrender to custody; or

    (b) commit an offence while on bail; or

    (c) interfere with witnesses or otherwise obstruct the course of justice . . . [46]

However, defendants may also find themselves remanded in custody if they are unwilling or unable to find sureties or security for their surrender to custody at the next hearing of their case or to comply with any conditions which the court chooses to attach to their release on bail.[47] In other words the magistrates, who have sole responsibility for granting or refusing bail, may decide to release a defendant subject to him providing some form of guarantee that he will appear at the court when required to do so and that he will behave himself until that time. Guarantees may take the form of a surety, that is a person who is prepared to vouch for the defendant and risk losing a sum of money if the defendant fails to appear, money security paid into court by the defendant, where the court believes there is a risk he might leave the country or conditions, such as reporting to the police regularly or surrendering his passport.

The magistrates have the power to grant or withhold bail at any stage during the process from first appearance to sentencing. Once a defendant has pleaded guilty, the magistrates may keep him in custody while reports are prepared simply on the ground that it it would otherwise be impractical.[48] This provision might apply, for example, where the magistrates want a full medical and psychiatric report and it seems unlikely that the defendant would attend hospital voluntarily.

Despite the extent of these powers, it is proportionately few defendants who find themselves in custody on remand. According to the official statistics for 1977, 81 per cent of defendants accused of indictable (more serious) offences were on bail throughout, while a further 6 per cent spent only part of their time, between first appearance and sentence or acquittal, in custody. The remaining 13 per cent spent the whole period in custody. The highest rates for denial of bail throughout the proceedings were to be found in cases of robbery (35 per cent), burglary (22 per cent), sexual offences (18 per cent), while the lowest rates were for criminal damage (11 per cent), violence against people (11 per cent) and handling stolen goods (9 per cent). Although it can be argued that different considerations apply to bail decisions than to sentencing, a recurrent jarring note in the criminal statistics is the fact that almost half those defendants whom magistrates remand in custody are subsequently given non-custodial sentences, giving rise to the suggestion that some magistrates may refuse bail as a punishment. Of those defendants who were granted bail by magistrates in 1977 only 3 per cent failed to attend court to face trial or sentence.

The results of research studies carried out before the Bail Act indicate quite clearly that it is only on rare occasions that magistrates refuse bail in the absence of objections to bail from the police.[49] These studies also found that whether or not the defendant had been on bail from the police station before appearing at the magistrates' court was a factor which correlated strongly with the granting or denial of bail by the magistrates. Apart from the nature of the offence, factors which appeared to reduce a defendant's chances of obtaining bail were residence outside the United Kingdom, lack of a fixed address and a long criminal record. On the other hand women were much more likely than men to obtain bail and the likelihood of being released for both sexes increased with the age of the defendant.[50] Only 3 per cent of the total number of defendants bailed by magistrates failed to appear at their trial. Defendants who have been refused bail by the magistrates may apply to a High Court judge. Those who can afford it may pay a lawyer to appear before the judge, while the remainder are obliged to apply in writing only through the Official Solicitor. The success rate in 1979 for 'paying' applicants was 30.6 per cent compared to 6.1 per cent for those applying through the Official Solicitor.[51]

Turning to the second of the two main pre-sentencing powers of magistrates' courts, the granting of legal aid, the exercise of this power, unlike that of bail, takes up very little court time. This is because the major part of the administration of the legal aid system is carried on behind the scenes in the court offices. It is here that the court clerks make the initial decision as to whether to grant legal aid to defendants who have submitted an application form and a statement of means. If they decide not to grant legal aid, they must pass the form and statement to a magistrate for further consideration.[52] The magistrate may then grant the application, refuse it or make the award of legal aid conditional on the defendant making a downpayment to the court. In theory a defendant may make as many applications for legal aid as he wishes. In addition to submitting and application form, he may also make an oral application in open court before a bench of magistrates. However, such applications are unusual. There is no appeal against refusal of legal aid except on the ground that the court has incorrectly assessed the defendant's needs.[53]

For most defendants the refusal of legal aid will mean that they will appear in court unrepresented, being unable or unwilling to meet the costs of instructing a solicitor privately. For those defendants who do obtain a legal aid order, their legal costs in all matters relating to the court proceedings, including advice and representation, the fees of expert witnesses and any other legal costs and expenses necessary in the preparation or presentation of the case together with advice on whether to appeal will be covered by the legal aid fund.

Generally, magistrates may grant or refuse applications for legal aid at will. The only statutory guidelines state that they may grant legal aid 'when it appears in the interests of justice' and when it appears that the defendant's means 'are such that he requires assistance in meeting' his legal costs.[54] However, the court is bound to offer the defendant legal aid in three instances: when he is accused of murder, when he may have to be remanded in custody either for a report to be prepared on him or having previously been refused bail at the magistrates' court[55] or where the magistrates are considering passing a custodial sentence and the defendant has not previously been sentenced to custodial punishment.[56] The only other guidance to magistrates as to how they should interpret and use their discretion comes from the Widgery Committee's recommendations[57] as to when legal aid should be granted and various Home Office circulars which in recent years have tended to encourage magistrates and clerks to economise in the granting of legal aid.[58] The exhortation to economise is perhaps not surprising when one considers that the cost of the criminal legal aid scheme increased seven-fold between 1969 and 1977 from £6 million to £43 million.[59]

The number of defendants who received legal aid orders also rose sharply after the introduction of a comprehensive criminal legal aid scheme in 1967 reaching a peak in the mid-seventies. As might be expected, given the extent of the magistrates' discretion, there is considerable variation both in the types of case for which legal aid is ordered and refused and between the policies of different magistrates' courts. According to the official statistics, for non-indictable (less serious offences) the defendant was represented under legal aid in only 1.8 per cent of cases in 1976, and the refusal rate for applications was 35 per cent. For indictable offences, however, legal aid was awarded in 52.9 per cent of cases and the refusal rate was only 8 per cent.[60] Variations between the refusal rates of different courts may be extreme even within a small geographical area. In 1977, for example, within the

Inner London area Hampstead magistrates' court had a refusal rate
for summary trials of 4 per cent compared with a rate of 47 per cent at
Highbury Corner, while a 5 per cent refusal rate at Dartford contrasts
with a 57 per cent rate at Highgate.[61] Attempts to obtain a High Court
order requiring magistrates to grant legal aid in cases which clearly
fell within the criteria laid down by the Widgery Committee have
failed, the judges being reluctant to interfere with the administrative
discretion of the magistrates.[62] Since magistrates are not obliged to
give any reasons for refusing a legal aid application, on can only
speculate as to the differences in attitude between different benches
which give rise to such wide variations in the way in which they choose
to exercise their powers, but it would appear that some magistrates
see themselves as guardians of the public coffers, while others consider
that saving the state money does not fall within their magisterial
duties. Moreover, some magistrates and clerks hold the view that lawyers help proceedings to run smoothly, while others see them as unnecessary time-wasters in most cases.

6. Defendants' Courtroom Rights

The formal process relates not only to the powers of those who make
decisions about defendants, but it concerns also the ability of defendants through the operation of the legal rules to influence the decisions
that are made about them. One important right of all defendants is
to be represented in court by a barrister or solicitor, although, as we
have seen, in very few situations does he have the right to insist that the
state assists him in paying for such representation. The combination of
legal aid, insurance and private funds has resulted in recent years in
just under half of all those who appear as defendants in magistrates'
courts being represented at some time between their first and final
appearances at court.[63] The likelihood of representation, of course,
increases as the case proceeds, so that far fewer than half have a lawyer
to speak for them at their first appearance. One study carried out in
1970 found that for non-motoring offences this figure was as low as 20
per cent.[64] However, the introduction of Duty Solicitor schemes at
many busy courts has almost certainly increased this proportion.

Another important right open to many, but not all, defendants
concerns the choice of venue. Some offences, the most serious and the
least serious, are triable respectively only on indictment, that is at the
Crown Court, or only summarily before the magistrates. Yet, there are

many others which are triable either way. Generally the defendant has the right to insist on trial by indictment in such cases, even if the prosecution and the magistrates prefer that the case be tried summarily.[65] Before making this choice the defendant has the right to be told in open court that, even if he chooses summary trial, the magistrates may send him to the Crown Court for sentencing if they consider that their powers of sentencing are insufficient.[66] Nevertheless the overwhelming majority of defendants who have a choice of venue choose summary trial. In one study carried out at Sheffield this figure was as high as 95 per cent.[67]

By pleading guilty a defendant effectively gives up his right to require the prosecution to prove its case against him. In order to avoid the risk of the defendant's plea being mis-represented to the court, he must personally announce his plea in open court, even if he has a lawyer in court to represent him.[68] Guilty pleaders have the right to question any evidence the prosecution might bring concerning the details of the offence, his involvement or his antecedents, that is his previous convictions and information about his social background. The defendant also has the right to address the court in mitigation, which means that he may draw the magistrates' attention to any matters concerning the offence or his circumstances which might influence them to treat him more leniently than they might otherwise have done had they merely received details of the offence and antecedents from the prosecution. The strict rules of evidence which apply to contested cases do not appear to operate in relation to pleas in mitigation, so the defendant may, for example, produce a letter from his employer or give the magistrates information about himself without any proof that this information is accurate.

7. Defence Lawyers

Where a defendant is legally represented, he effectively passes his right to question witnesses and plead in mitigation to his barrister or solicitor. He must remain silent while his lawyer does all the talking. Where the lawyer has been instructed privately, the defendant will pay an agreed fee for his services, usually payable in advance. Lawyers operating under the criminal legal aid scheme, however, receive no money direct from their clients. Instead, they submit their *pro forma* bill to the Legal Aid Area Secretary after the case is over and he assesses it, either accepting the amount asked for or reducing it. In cases where it is reduced, the solicitor who submitted the bill may appeal to the Legal Aid Area Committee, which consists of other lawyers.[69] The solicitor's charges reflect not the skill and expertise he puts into his work, nor the success or failure of his efforts, but purely and simply the amount of time he has spent on the case, including time travelling between the court and his office and time spent sitting around waiting for the case to be called. A London solicitor recently revealed that during the course of four weeks' work in the magistrates' courts he had spent 28 hours 55 minutes waiting for cases to be heard at some considerable cost to the legal aid fund.[70]

8. The Sentencing Powers of Magistrates

Although the general principles of flexibility and individualisation have acted as guiding lights for sentencing by magistrates' courts, there have been several attempts through the formal rules to limit magisterial discretion. The main objective in trying to control sentencers is to achieve consistency between different courts and different benches of magistrates sitting at the same court. The second objective might be to prevent magistrates being too severe or too lenient in certain types of offences or for certain categories of offender. These attempts to restrict magistrates' discretion have usually been foisted upon an unwilling magistracy. In one recent instance, the magistrates' resentment actually succeeded in having removed from the statute book a requirement to suspend all prison sentences passed on defendants who had not previously received a custodial sentence.[71] At present the penalties available to magistrates when dealing with offenders range from an absolute discharge to a sentence of imprisonment, usually for no more than six months, but, for a few offences, up to a year. Magistrates may also impose a fine of up to £1,000. There are various ways in which their discretion in the use of these powers may be restricted.

The use of mandatory sentences in magistrates' courts is confined to motoring offences. The most controversial and widely known of these is disqualification for the offence of driving with excess alcohol. This is clearly a safeguard against leniency. There are also semi-mandatory provisions which lay down what the sentence ought to be in normal circumstances, but then go on to allow the magistrates to refrain from imposing that sentence if there are 'special reasons' or 'exceptional circumstances' or if it would be 'unjust'. One of these provisions arises when an offence has been committed by a person who has previously received a suspended sentence. Another occurs in 'totting up' cases for road traffic offences. It would seem that this latter semi-mandatory provision is not particularly effective in producing consistency in sentencing. Many are the times when an eloquent plea in mitigation has persuaded the magistrates' bench not to disqualify the defendant from driving. One recent study of 717 cases dealt with over 6 months shows that an average of 31 per cent of the motorists involved were not disqualified and in one court this figure was as high as 54 per cent.[72] Even requiring the magistrates to put forward their reasons for not implementing a penalty does not seem to make the statutory provisions more effective, for the magistrates may simply put down the standard entry such as 'undue hardship' without giving any further indication of the court's thinking.[73] In addition to prohibited sentences, mandatory sentences and semi-mandatory sentences, there are statutory exhortations. For example, the imprisonment of an offender of under 21 years of age is expressly discouraged except as a last resort, when no other methods of dealing with the offender are appropriate.[74] Similarly, committal for sentence to the Crown Court is open to magistrates only on the basis of the defendant's character and antecedents and not on the gravity of the offence.[75] Furthermore, a suspended sentence should, according to the statutory guidelines, be imposed only where a prison sentence is appropriate and should not be a substitute for a fine.[76] Once again, considerable doubt has been expressed as to the effectiveness of these exhortations.

Other controls over magistrates' sentencing include the system of appeals to the Crown Court and Court of Appeal. Yet the results of Crown Court appeals are not published in any systematic way, so that even the bench of magistrates responsible for the original sentence might well be ignorant of the fact that their decision was disapproved on appeal. Court of Appeal decisions on the other hand are publicised in *The Magistrate,* the journal of the Magistrates' Association, in the Criminal Law Review and in books such as Thomas's *Principles of Sentencing.*[77] Yet again, however, there is no sure way of ensuring that individual magistrates read these appellate decisions or have them drawn to their attention. From time to time the Magistrates' Association do issue guidelines on 'appropriate penalties', but these do not usually extend beyond motoring offences.[78] While the Home Office produces a handbook entitled, *The Sentence of the Court.*[79]

Despite all these attempts to achieve a measure of consistency, such studies as have been carried out on the sentencing practices of magistrates' courts indicate that there are wide variations between different courts. Roger Hood almost 20 years ago made a detailed study of property offences in 12 courts. He found that the use of prison for these offences varied from 15 per cent to 50 per cent, probation from 1 per cent to 24 per cent, fines from 25 per cent to 84 per cent and discharge from 6 per cent to 19 per cent.[80] Over the years various explanations have been offered for these discrepancies between the sentencing of different courts. Those explanations most often favoured by defenders of the magistrates' courts system have been differences in the backgrounds of offenders and the types of offences that different courts have to deal with or differences in local conditions such as a spate of shoplifting in a particular town which might influence the magistrates to use heavy sentences as a deterrent measure. However, a recent Home Office study of 30 courts found that differences between courts' sentencing patterns were only partly attributable to differences in the types of offence and characteristics of offenders. Moreover, the author of this study dismissed as lacking any supporting evidence 'the notion that for reasons of deterrence, severity of sentencing is a response to a crime problem'.[81] The report accepted that variations in police cautioning from area to area might affect the type of offender appearing before the court and that in turn could result in differences in sentencing practices. It also suggested that differences in probation resources from area to area might account in part for discrepancies in the use of probation orders. However, such explanations did not provide a complete explanation for such large variations in the use of imprisonment as 3 per cent of all adult, male indictable offenders in one court to 19 per cent in another, or in the use of fines from 46 per cent in one court to 76 per cent in another.[82] What seemed to be a major factor is variations in sentencing traditions at different courts and the absence of any attempt at most courts to take any account of the sentencing policies of other magistrates' courts, even of their neighbouring courts. The author of this study concluded: 'Indeed one could if one wished see the insularity and durability of court traditions as major obstacles to attaining greater consistency between courts.'[83] Why such traditions exist and how they are explained are discussed in the next chapter. The full range of powers that magistrates may exercise are set out below. However, not all these provisions are available to the magistrates for every offence. Some statutory offences restrict the magistrates' powers by limiting the term of prison or the amount of the fine that may be imposed.

When the magistrates consider that their powers of sentencing are insufficient, they may commit the defendant to the Crown Court for sentencing under section 29, Magistrates' Courts Act 1952 (as amended). Moreover, where the magistrates are minded to recommend a borstal sentence for an offender aged between 17 and 21, they must commit him to the Crown Court as they themselves have no power to impose a borstal sentence.[84] In 1977 4,828 adult offenders were committed to the Crown Court for sentence. In about half these cases, however, the Crown Court decided upon a sentence which was less than the maximum the magistrates could have imposed.[85]

The full range of powers that a magistrates' court can exercise are as follows (the maximum sentence for any particular offence is set out in the statute creating the offence; e.g. Theft Act 1968):

Absolute and Conditional Discharge

These powers are to be used where it is inexpedient to inflict punishment.[86] An Absolute Discharge can be used if, in the circumstances, the offence was too trivial and technical to make deterrence, retribution or rehabilitation necessary. In this case the convicted person simply leaves the court and no further action can be taken for the offence. However, if the court feels that a mild individual deterrent may be useful it can make a conditional discharge. Under this the offender is faced with the threat that, for a specified period up to three years, if he is convicted again he could be sentenced again for the first offence. In 1977 9 per cent of male offenders and 20 per cent of female offenders were dealt with by absolute and conditional discharge.[87]

Binding Over

In addition a court can bind the offender over to keep the peace and be of good behaviour, requiring him to enter into a recognisance with or without sureties which can be forfeited if he fails to keep the peace even if he doesn't actually commit an offence. Since 1361[88] they have had the power to bind over anyone appearing before them (even a witness).

Attendance Centre Orders

These can be made to male offenders under the age of 21, provided they live near an appropriate centre. They are intended to be both deterrent in causing loss of leisure and inconvenience and reformative in teaching 'the constructive use of leisure'.[89] However there are only two centres for those over 17, so attendance centre orders are not numerically important for sentencing in adult criminal courts.

Community Service Orders

Under ss. 14–17 of the Powers of Criminal Courts Act 1973 the courts can order that offenders aged 17 and over can be ordered to perform specific unpaid work of benefit to the community for between 40 and 240 hours over a period of 12 months, provided the offender agrees and suitable arrangements can be made. It has been described as being suitable for 'offenders whose offences show a certain degree of selfish disregard for the community without causing substantial injury'.[90] It is mostly used for young offenders and is supervised by a probation officer. In 1977 2 per cent of male offenders and 1 per cent of female offenders were given Community Service orders.

Probation

The official aims of probation are to re-establish the offender as a responsible member of the community and to keep a watchful eye on him and so protect society. The court releases him on condition that he visits a probation officer at regular specified intervals for between one and three years. In 1977 70 per cent of offenders put on probation were given probation for between one and two years.[91] The court can attach conditions to the order, e.g. that the offender be of good behaviour and lead an industrious life, that he lives in a probation hostel for a year, that he should attend a day training centre or that he should receive psychiatric treatment.[92]

The offender will breach if he either fails to comply with one of the conditions of it or if he commits a further offence. In the latter case he may be sentenced for the original offence, and in the former he can be fined, given an attendance centre or community service order, or sentenced for the original offence. Thus it should be noted that the court can use sanctions to control the offender's behaviour even though he does not actually commit a further offence. In 1977 5 per cent of male offenders and 12 per cent of female offenders were given probation orders. The percentages for both have declined in recent years.[93]

Fine

The fine is the most common sentence used by the courts to deal with 53 per cent of male offenders and 57 per cent of female offenders found guilty of indictable offences. It is used even more for non-indictable offences. In 1977 98 per cent of offenders sentenced by magistrates' courts for motoring offences and 91 per cent sentenced by magistrates' courts for other non-indictable offences were fined. In total 1,713,862 people were fined by magistrates' courts in 1977.[94]

Fines made for indictable offences by magistrates' courts for offenders over 16 are generally of the £10–£30 range, the most common amount being from £21–£30. In 1977 60 per cent of male offenders and 70 per cent of female offenders were given fines of £30 or less, and 86 per cent of male offenders and 90 per cent of female offenders were given fines of £50 or less.[95] The maximum fine that magistrates' courts can give is £400 with a very few exceptions. Although magistrates are supposed to take into account the means of the offender in fixing the amount of the fine, there is no explicit formula relating the fine to his income.

Imprisonment

The magistrates' ultimate sanction is to deprive the offender of his liberty. The maximum sentence they can pass is six months imprisonment for one offence, or twelve months for more than one offence.[96] In sending to a gaol an adult offender who has not been imprisoned before, the court must be of opinion that no other method of dealing with him is appropriate taking into account both the circumstance of the offence and of the offender. It must also record its reasons for doing so.[97]

A court imposing a sentence of imprisonment for two years or less may decide to suspend the sentence by ordering that it will not come into effect if the offender commits no further offences for a stated period. This is seen as a last chance and must not be used unless 'a sentence of imprisonment would have been appropriate in the absence of any power to suspend such a sentence'.[98] If a further offence is committed, the suspended sentence must be brought into effect except in special circumstances.

In 1977 17 per cent of male offenders and 3 per cent of female offenders found guilty of indictable offences were sentenced to immediate imprisonment while a further 12 per cent and 6 per cent respectively were given suspended sentences.[99] Over recent years the use of imprisonment has declined. The proportion of male offenders found guilty of indictable offences given immediate or suspended sentences has fallen from 35 per cent in 1968 to 29 per cent in 1977.[100]

Borstal Training

This is exclusively for young offenders aged between 15 and 21, and is the normal method of custodial treatment for offenders within this age group. Borstal training is generally designed to be more reformative than prison, although there are a very wide range of regimes from something like boarding school to something more like 'prison'. Magistrates' courts have no power (with one exception) to send offenders to borstal themselves but may commit them to the Crown Court for sentence with a recommendation for borstal training under s. 28 of the Magistrates' Courts Act 1952.

Detention Centre

Male offenders between 14 and 21 may be sent to a Detention Centre for from 3–6 months for a period of rigorous discipline and training. The success rate however, as measured by the proportion of offenders reconvicted within three years, has proved disappointing. In fact this sentence is rarely used these days in respect of offenders over the age of 16.

Additional Powers

Magistrates have an overriding power to defer the passing of sentence on an offender for a maximum period of six months, after which time they may have regard to his conduct after conviction or to any changes in his circumstances. Although this book is not concerned with mentally abnormal offenders, it is worth mentioning that the magistrates have powers under the Mental Health Act 1959 to make hospital orders where two doctors have certified that the offender is suffering from a mental illness. Similarly, we are not directly concerned with people charged with minor motoring offences and magistrates, in addition to fining the offender, may endorse his licence and disqualify him in certain circumstances. It should also be mentioned, however, that disqualification from driving may be imposed as a penalty for what are normally regarded as 'crimes' where a motor vehicle was involved in the offence, such as taking and driving a car without the owner's permission.

9. Social Enquiry and Other Reports

No matter how serious or how trivial the offence, the magistrates may, at their discretion, require the Probation Service to prepare and submit a social enquiry report on the offender. Where they are considering making a probation order or passing a sentence of imprisonment or detention centre or making a recommendation for borstal training, the use of such reports is recommended by statute, but failure to call for a report before passing sentence does not invalidate the sentence.[101]

The number of social enquiry reports made has increased steadily over the years. By 1966 the numbers of reports had increased to 294 per cent of the 1956 level and by 1971 the number had increased to 466 per cent of the 1956 level in adult cases in magistrates' courts. By 1971 17 per cent of adult indictable offenders in magistrates' courts had social enquiry reports made on them before sentencing.[102] However since then the rate of increase has tended to level off. In 1976 a total of 106,724 social enquiry reports were made on adults.[103] In addition to social enquiry reports, the magistrates may ask for medical reports as to both the defendant's physical and mental health. Whenever the magistrates ask for reports, they may order that the defendant should be kept in custody where it would be impracticable to complete the enquiries or make the report without keeping him in custody. In the case of medical reports, the custodial remand has been severely criticised on the ground that it is often unnecessary to keep someone in a prison or remand centre for as long as four weeks where the interview or examination on which the report is based often takes no longer than an hour.[104]

10. Offences taken into Consideration

Before sentence, a defendant may ask the court to take into consideration other offences which he admits, but for which he has not been convicted (called 't-i-cs'). In such cases the police produce a list signed by the defendant of all the cases he admits. The advantage to the police is that these crimes can now be classified as 'cleared up', while the defendant benefits from the fact that the magistrates may not give him a more severe sentence than the maximum permitted for the offence for which he has been convicted. However, they may, of course, commit him to the Crown Court for sentencing on the basis that their own powers are insufficient given all the circumstances of the case.

11. Costs, Contributions and Compensation

Having sentenced a defendant, the magistrates may, unless his means are very low or he is drawing Supplementary Benefit,[105] order him to pay a contribution towards his legal aid costs.[106] Although the magistrates usually refer to a defendant's statement of means before making a 'contribution order', they have an absolute discretion as to the amount they consider appropriate and the time limit in which it should be paid. They may also order him to pay the costs of the prosecution or such an amount towards the prosecution costs as they think 'just and reasonable'.[107] Such orders for costs may be made even where the defendant is in receipt of a legal aid order. It was emphasised in one appellate court case that an order for costs should be made only to pay the prosecution expenses and should not be used as a disguised punishment for the offence.

Finally, the magistrates may order any convicted person to compensate the victim of his crime and restore any property he may have taken. Compensation must take the form of monetary payments, but these may be ordered not merely in cases where the victim has suffered financial loss, but also where physical injuries have been inflicted on him. Within the limits laid down by statute, the magistrates have an absolute discretion as to how much compensation to order.[108]

12. Appeals against Sentence

The Magistrates' Courts Act 1952 s.83 (as subsequently amended)[109] gives all defendants convicted of offences in the magistrates' courts a right to appeal to the Crown Court against sentence (and against conviction for those who pleaded not guilty). However to this must be added the exception that defendants cannot appeal against a probation order, which technically does not count as a 'sentence' (and which in any case the defendant consented to), or conditional discharges. The Crown Court has the power to confirm, reverse or vary any decision of the magistrates, and (unlike appeals to the Court of Appeal) can give a more severe punishment than the original sentence provided that it is one that the magistrates' court could have given.[110]

Only a tiny proportion of defendants use their right to appeal: about 1.4 per cent of those sentenced for indictable offences and less than 1 per cent of those sentenced for non-indictable offences.[111] This is despite the fact that in 1977 about half of all appellants (including those appealing against conviction) had their sentences quashed or varied, and the power to vary sentences upward is very rarely used.

Notes

1. *Criminal Statistics 1977* (HMSO, London), Table 1.
2. Ibid., Table 5.1
3. See A.E. Bottoms and J.D. McClean, *Defendants — The Criminal Process*. Routledge and Kegan Paul, London, (1976), Table 3.3, p. 75.
4. Misuse of Drugs Act 1971, s. 23(2).
5. Firearms Act 1968, s. 4.7.
6. e.g. Metropolitan Police Act 1839, s. 66.
7. Protection of Birds Act 1967.
8. P. Laurie, *Scotland Yard* (Penguin, Harmondsworth, 1972).
9. Magistrates' Court Act 1952, s. 40.
10. Mental Health Act 1959, part IV.
11. Immigration Act 1971, s. 2.
12. *Rice* v. *Connolly* [1966] 3 W.L.R. 17; Road Traffic Act 1972 s. 162.
13. *R.* v. *Priestly* (1965) 51 Cr. App. Rep.1.
14. See M. King (ed.), *Guilty until Proved Innocent* (Release Lawyers, London, 1973), p. 37.
15. See generally S. Kadish and M. Paulson, *Criminal Law and its Processes*, 3rd edn (Little Brown, Boston, 1975), Ch. 12.
16. Bottoms and McClean *Defendants*, p. 115.
17. Home Office Circular no. 31/1964.
18. Ibid.
19. M. Zander, 'Access to a Solicitor in the Police Station', *Criminal Law Review* (1972), pp. 342-50; J. Baldwin and M. McConville, 'Police Interrogation and the Right to See a Solicitor', *Criminal Law Review* (1979), pp. 143-52.
20. *R.* v. *Allen* [1977] Criminal Law Review, p. 163
21. *R.* v. *Elliot* [1977] Criminal Law Review, p. 551; *R.* v. *Lemsatef* [1977] 2 All E.R. 385.
22. [1972] 1 All E.R. 114 at p. 118.
23. Criminal Law Act 1977, s. 62, see pp. 241-8.
24. See pp. 141-8.
25. Criminal Law Act 1967, s. 2(3). In addition to this general statutory power there is a Common Law power to arrest where a breach of the peace might take place or has been committed and is likely to continue, and also various specific powers under various different statutes, e.g. poaching at night, failure to pay for or show a railway ticket.
26. *R.* v. *Inwood* [1973] I. W.L.R. 647.
27. *Christie* v. *Leachinsky* [1947] A.C. 573.
28. Magistrates' Courts Act 1952, s. 1. The rules relating to arrest and detention are different if the defendant is under 17.
29. Magistrates' Court Act 1952, s. 38(4).
30. Preamble to the Judges' Rules.
31. Magistrates' Court Act 1952, s. 31(1).
32. *Hussein* v. *Choong Fooh Kum* [1970] A.C. 442.
33. See T. Gifford and P. O'Connor, 'Habeas Corpus', *Legal Action Group Bulletin* (1979), p. 182.
34. Administration of Justice Act 1973, s. 21.
35. In the Duchy of Lancaster the appointment of magistrates is the responsibility of the Chancellor of the Duchy of Lancaster.
36. See *Royal Commission on the Selection of Justices of the Peace*, Cd. 2865 (HMSO, London, 1910).
37. J. Baldwin, 'The Social Composition of the Magistracy', *British Journal of*

58 *The Framework of Criminal Justice*

Criminology, vol. 16, no. 2 (1976), pp. 171–4.

38. Baldwin, ibid.

39. House of Commons Written Answers, Hansard 3rd Feb. col. 434.

40. D. Bartlett and J. Walker, 'Making Benches — The Inner Wheel', *New Society* (19 April 1973), p. 145. See also 'Wheel of Influence', *New Society* (25 December 1975), by the same authors.

41. R. Hood, *Sentencing the Motoring Offender* (Heinemann, London, 1972), p. 53.

42. Baldwin, 'The Social Composition of the Magistracy'.

43. J. Baldwin. 'The Compulsory Training of Magistrates', *Criminal Law Review* (1975), p. 634.

44. See Lord Goddard's judgment in *R.* v. *East Kerrier Justices, ex parte* Mundy [1952] 2 All E.R. 144.

45. Letter to the author from the Home Office dated 12 August 1976.

46. Bail Act 1976, Schedule I, Part I, s. 2. Where the defendant is charged with a non-imprisonable offence, the magistrates may refuse bail only if he has previously absconded and they believe that this is likely to recur (Part II, s. 2).

47. Bail Act, s. 5.

48. Bail Act, Schedule I, Part I, s. 7.

49. M. King, *Bail or Custody* (Cobden Trust, London, 1971), p. 30.

50. F. Simon and M. Weatheritt, *The Use of Bail and Custody by London Magistrates before and after the Criminal Justice Act 1967* (HMSO, London, 1974), p. 21.

51. P. Cavadino, 'Bail Applications by Remand Prisoners', *New Law Journal,* 1980, pp. 661-2.

52. Legal Aid in Criminal Proceedings (General) Regulations (1968) Reg. 1.6.

53. There is the possibility of a Judicial Review by the High Court but these are rarely successful in altering magistrates' decisions.

54. Legal Aid Act 1974, s. 28.

55. Bail Act 1976, s. 11.

56. Powers of the Criminal Courts Act 1973, s. 21.

57. Widgery (ch.) *Report of the Departmental Committee on Legal Aid in Criminal Proceedings* Cmnd. 2934 (HMSO, London, 1966).

58. Home Office Circular, Hoc 97/7978.

59. *The 27th Legal Aid and Advice Report, 1976-7* (HMSO, London 1977).

60. *Criminal Statistics 1977.*

61. H. Levinson, 'Legal Aid in Summary Proceedings in Magistrates' Courts Revisited', *New Law Journal* (1979), p. 375.

62. See Legal Action Group Bulletin (1979), p. 375.

63. M. King, 'Magistrates Courts Surveyed', *Rights,* vol. 1, no. 1 (1976), p. 11.

64. M. King, *Bail or Custody,* p. 30.

65. Criminal Law Act 1977.

66. *R.* v. *Kent Justices, ex parte* Machin [1952] 1 All E.R. 1123.

67. Bottoms and McClean, *Defendants,* p. 78.

68. *R.* v. *Wakefield Justices, ex parte* Butterworths [1970] All E.R. 1181.

69. Legal Aid in Criminal Proceedings (General) Regulations 1968.

70. B. Nash reported in E. Burney, *J.P. — Magistrate, Court and Community* (Hutchinson, London, 1979), p. 24.

71. Criminal Justice Act 1967 and Criminal Justice Act 1972.

72. Burney, *J.P.,* p. 132.

73. Ibid., p. 133.

74. Powers of the Criminal Courts Act 1973, s. 20.

75. Magistrates' Courts Act 1952, s. 29.

76. Powers of the Criminal Courts Act 1973, s. 22(2).

77. D. Thomas, *Principles of Sentencing* (Heinemann, London, 1979).

78. e.g. The Magistrates' Association, 'Suggestions for Traffic Offence Penalties', *The Magistrate* (1978).

79. (HMSO, London, 1978.)

80. R. Hood, *Sentencing in Magistrates' Courts* (Stevens, London, 1962).

81. R. Tarling, *Sentencing Practice in Magistrates' Courts,* Home Office Research Study No. 56 (HMSO, London, 1979), Ch. 4.

82. Ibid., Ch. 7.

83. Ibid., p. 45.

84. *Criminal Statistics 1977,* Table 1(a).

85. Ibid., p. 118.

86. Criminal Justice Act 1948, s. 7.

87. *Criminal Statistics 1977,* Table 6.3.

88. Justice of the Peace Act 1361.

89. Ingelby (ch.), *Report of the Committee on Children and Young Persons,* Cmnd. 1191 (HMSO, London, 1960).

90. D. Barnard, *The Criminal Court in Action* (Butterworths, London, 1974), p. 141.

91. *Criminal Statistics 1977,* p. 106.

92. Powers of the Criminal Courts Act 1973. ss. 3 & 4.

93. *Criminal Statistics 1977,* Table 6.3.

94. Ibid., Table 6.6.

95. Ibid., Table 6.13.

96. Magistrates' Courts Act 1952, s. 108 (2).

97. Powers of the Criminal Courts Act 1973, s. 19.

98. Ibid., s. 22.

99. *Criminal Statistics 1977,* Table 6.2.

100. Ibid., Table 6.2.

101. Powers of the Criminal Courts Act 1973, s. 45(3).

102. M. Davies, 'Social Enquiry Reports for the Courts', *British Journal of Criminology,* vol. 4(1974), p. 18.

103. J. Thorpe, *Social Enquiry Reports* (HMSO, London 1979), footnote p. 13.

104. *Home Office Working Party: Bail Procedures in Magistrates' Courts* (HMSO, London, 1974) pp. 53-6.

105. Legal Aid in Criminal Proceedings (Assessment of Resources) Regulations 1978, Reg. 7(2).

106. Legal Aid Act 1974. s. 29(3).

107. Costs in Criminal Cases Act 1973, s. 2.

108. Powers of the Criminal Courts Act 1973, s. 35.

109. Courts Act 1971, Schedule 9.

110. Ibid.

111. *Criminal Statistics 1977,* Table 6.6.

Scenes in the Criminal Justice Process

Many works on the criminal justice process, both textbooks and research studies, do not go much further than an examination of the formal rules and statistics concerning the operation of these rules. Yet, stopping one's analysis at this point provides almost no information about the way in which those concerned with actually putting the formal system of rules into practice interpret their roles and relate to the defendant and to one another. Furthermore, it may help to give the misleading impression that it is the formal rules which preoccupy the participants and determine the nature of their roles. Thus policemen and defence lawyers are always seen as antagonists, barristers and solicitors always serve their clients' best interests, court clerks are simply legal advisers to the lay magistrates and probation officers are sentencing experts. This ignores any other forces which may be influencing the behaviour of these participants.

In turn, this formalistic level of analysis leads to a somewhat mechanistic approach to attempts to understand and improve the criminal justice system. The student of criminal justice, rather like a clock-repairer, looks at the cogs and wheels of the system to see if the rules are being followed and the roles played out according to a formalised script. If the rules are not being followed or if the reality of the system's operation does not conform with the formal expectations, then, like a clock, the system has gone wrong and requires repairs or adjustment. According to this approach, therefore, research into criminal justice and the application of the results of this research together represent a concentrated attempt to bring the system into line with the idealised notion of criminal justice which is supposedly contained in the formal rules.

Allied to this mechanistic approach is the tendency to concentrate upon easily observable and readily available aspects of the system's operation. After all, it is comparatively easy for 'interpreters' from outside, be they journalists or academic researchers, to obtain information about such officially recorded facts as the proportion of legal aid applications refused by each court, the numbers granted bail and the percentage of offenders receiving a suspended sentence. They may also with little effort analyse and criticise the decisions and arguments set down in the law reports of appeal cases. Much more difficult is discovering what goes on in what one might call the 'low visibility' areas of the system, that is those activities, often crucial to the final outcome of the case, which take place away from the public gaze and which are not recorded in the official statistics of the law reports. Finding out about these areas requires either actual involvement as a participant in the process or, for the outsider, long and difficult research. These low visibility areas include police interrogations, the interviews between lawyers and their clients and between probation officers and the subjects of social enquiry reports, and plea-bargaining and other negotiations between the courtroom professionals. In this chapter I have attempted to depart as far as possible from the formal, mechanistic approach and to concentrate upon evidence concerning the criminal justice system in magistrates' courts which is not readily available to the journalist or the lazy researcher. Fortunately, I am assisted in this exercise by several researchers who have recently produced systematic evidence about what happens 'behind the scenes' of criminal justice. Indeed, if this chapter had been written only five years ago, I should have had to rely very much upon my own experience as a solicitor in the magistrates' court.

The 'scenes' that this chapter describes are as follows:

1. At the police station.
2. Waiting to be heard.
3. Being represented by a lawyer under legal aid.
4. Favours, negotiations and bargains.
5. Being the subject of a social enquiry report.
6. At the court.
7. Being sentenced.
8. Having one's name in the papers.

Together they cover most of the situations likely to be experienced by defendants who plead guilty in magistrates' courts. They should also provide the reader with some insight into the way in which pre-court events play a part in determining the nature of the courtroom hearing and in influencing the sentencing decision. The one omission from this list which might surprise some readers is the bail hearing. My reason for excluding this 'scene' relates to the concern expressed in Chapter 1 and reinforced at the beginning of this chapter that the study should as far as possible be directed away from formal notions of justice and injustice and mechanistic evaluations of the system 'going right' or 'going wrong'. To introduce a discussion of bail decisions would, I believe, be running the risk of raising just those issues which serve as distractions to the main objectives of this work.

1. At the Police Station

To provide incontrovertible evidence about the ways in which police action may influence the decision to plead guilty is a difficult task. The reluctance of policemen to bear witness to their own persuasive activities means that such evidence usually has to come from defendants themselves. Understandably, there is much resistance to accepting the word of defendants who plead guilty and are hence branded as criminals, while those defendants who contest the charges against them in court often have a vested interest in the accounts they give as to what happened to them at the police station, for these accounts are usually presented with a view to persuading the court to reject their written or oral confessions. However, it is now possible through the sheer weight of repetition by numerous defendants giving very similar accounts of their treatment at the hands of the police to build up a fairly accurate picture of police practices.

The authors of the Sheffield study, for example, found that 4 per cent of their sample of 1,207 guilty pleaders made allegations that the police had in some sense 'forced' them to confess.[1] They illustrate their finding with three cases where the defendants they interviewed made such allegations:

Case 2043 The defendant, aged 17, grabbed a woolly cap off a 13-year-old boy in the crowd going away from a football match. He said it was in fun, but a policeman has spotted him and he was taken to the station to be charged with theft. He claimed that the police had used violence on him and forced him to sign a statement, after which he had no choice but to plead guilty.

Case 1034 'I admitted possession. If I hadn't, they would have charged me with supplying. I had no choice: they threatened me and knocked me against the wall. I admitted having the stuff as I was so scared.'

Case 2080 (Charged with attempting to siphon petrol from a car in garage forecourt.) 'They were going to keep me in all night, and it would have been remand in custody next day. Also they said they'd accuse my friend, who's on a suspended sentence — so I admitted it.'

This picture has been reinforced and details have been added by defence solicitors who regularly attend police stations, by researchers such as Maureeen Cain [2] and Peter Laurie[3] who spent considerable time studying the police, by policemen who have retired or resigned from the force and by the occasional unguarded statement of serving police officers, usually intended for internal police consumption. But before we examine this picture, it is worth while asking why it is that the police should wish to persuade defendants to plead guilty in the first place.

There are various reasons all related to the organisational structure of the police force and the nature of police work. Before discussing these in detail, it is perhaps necessary to state what may seem to be an obvious fact — that the quickest, cheapest, easiest way for the police to secure convictions in court is for the defendant to plead guilty. There are even many cases where the police would most probably have been unable to obtain a conviction were it not for the defendant's admission of guilt. Furthermore, the surest precursor to a guilty plea is a confession. Peter Laurie[4] in his study of Scotland Yard estimated that every case where a defendant did not confess involved the detective an average two weeks extra work. Guilty pleas, then, lighten the policeman's load, but they do much more than that. According to Laurie again, 'a [guilty] plea pulls down the curtain on all past transactions. No questions can arise about the information that led to the arrest, about the arrest itself. There can be no complaints about the arresting officer's behaviour and no haggling over the Judges' Rules.'[5] In a contested case, by contrast, the police officer runs the risk of an acquittal and this may be seen as an implied criticism of his judgement and his work in preparing the case for trial. Yet this is not all he risks. In an increasing number of cases defendants today are challenging in court the police account of the events which led to their arrest or complaining that the officers concerned acted improperly, by exceeding their powers even to the extent of assaulting the defendant. Both acquittals and allegations of improper conduct are hardly likely to enhance a police officer's reputation. A conviction following a guilty plea, on the other hand, both helps the individual officer in his quest for promotion and reassures him of his own competence and at the same time of the worth of his job. There is ample reason, therefore, for policemen to try to persuade suspects to plead guilty and if possible to tie up the outcome of the court case by extracting written confessions from them.

As far as police methods of achieving these objectives are concerned, there is sufficient evidence to suggest that the following techniques are in current use:

(a) Disorienting the suspect by the speed and surprise of the arrest and detention.

(b) Controlling all information that the suspect receives while in custody by refusing to allow him to contact his solicitor and denying access to that solicitor should he arrive at the police station.[6]

(c) Leaving the suspect alone in a cell for long periods.

(d) Submitting the suspect to insults and displays of anger followed almost immediately by a show of sympathy and understanding.

(e) Submitting the suspect to prolonged, intensive questioning; going over the same ground over and over again in order to confuse the suspect into making errors and giving inconsistent answers.

(f) Giving the impression that the police have total control over the present situation and the future disposal of the suspects by the court, in particular threatening to have the suspect detained in custody for a long period or offering him the prospect of a lenient sentence.

(g) Threatening to involve members of the suspect's family or his friends if he does not confess.

(h) Impressing upon him his own worthlessness and the trouble he has caused and will cause to others, particularly to members of his family.

(i) Giving the suspect the impression that the evidence against him is much stronger than it actually is and convincing him that his confession is therefore a formality.

(j) Suggesting that there was a good reason for his having committed the deed, that he has too much intelligence to have done it without rhyme or reason, for example, in the case of sex crimes, explaining that sex-hunger is one of the strongest instincts motivating our lives. In the case of theft, suggesting that the suspect may have been hungry or deprived of the necessities of life.[7]

This is not to suggest that methods of this sort are necessarily employed in every case. Sometimes the police have water-tight evidence, which makes it unnecessary for them to obtain confessions. Many people are caught red-handed or confess spontaneously without any police pressure, often in order to relieve feelings of guilt or in the hope that a confession will shorten their ordeal.[8] Nor is the interrogation process always one-sided with the suspect playing the role of a passive victim. A suspect who is experienced in the ways of the system may often use his knowledge to gain advantages for himself. When the police are short of evidence, for example, he may exchange his guilty plea in return for some concession from the police such as a reduced charge, release on bail, help in framing his confession in a way calculated to attract the sympathy of the magistrates or the promise of a 'good word' from the prosecution in court.

It is impossible to predict exactly what is likely to happen to a particular suspect at the hands of the police, but certain variables which affect police attitudes and hence police action may usefully be identified. In the first place there is the police perception of the sort of person they are dealing with. Policemen, like many other social groups who encounter the general public during the course of their work, tend to reduce people to coarse stereotypes based upon sex, race, nationality and social class. Maureen Cain, in her study of the police, writes that immigrants (including Irish), were 'subject to stereotyping and abuse'. 'Niggers' were for example seen as 'in the main. . . pimps and layabouts living off what we pay in taxes'.[9] Secondly, the nature of the offence which the police are investigating could also affect their approach in dealing with the suspect. Obviously, a suspected murderer could expect very different treatment from a suspected petty shoplifter: although the police are likely to use the same sorts of techniques in both cases, the amount of time and effort the officers will be prepared to devote to breaking the suspect's resistance will be very different. In the third place, the strength of the police evidence before they bring in their suspect may also make a considerable difference to the way they handle him. The value of a confession diminishes in a direct counter-relationship to the persuasiveness of the other evidence against the suspect. Forensic evidence, such as finger-prints which inextricably link the suspect to the crime, will, for instance, reduce the need for a confession and hence for the police to put pressure on the suspect. However, even where strong evidence exists, it may still be necessry to persuade the suspect to talk in order, for example, to identify accomplices and discover where stolen property has been hidden. Finally, such characteristics of the suspect as his previous experience of police interrogation, his skills at bargaining, his possession of information which the police want, his familiarity with law, the rules of evidence and the extent of police powers may play and important part in determining exactly how the encounter between him and the police at the police station progresses. In a study of Holloway prisoners who pleaded guilty in court despite maintaining their innocence when interviewed at the prison after the case had been heard, the author stated that 'perhaps the most disturbing feature about the inconsistent pleaders was the number of women among them who had no previous convictions'.[10] The majority of these gave police advice or pressure as their reason for pleading guilty.

> Some of them said that the police had threatened that they would be 'sent down' if they pleaded not guilty; others said that they had been told that they would 'get off' (with a fine or probation etc.) if they did not contest the case. Several girls said that they had been advised to plead guilty in a kindly, even fatherly spirit, the policemen telling them that this was the simplest way to get the case over, and to avoid the risk of publicity, or remands in custody.[11]

Furthermore, the incidence among recidivist offenders who gave police advice or pressure as their reason for pleading 'inconsistently' was very much lower than for first offenders. The author remarks that 'It was easy to see how those without experience of police stations or courts might gratefully accept such [police] advice.'[12]

2. Waiting to be Heard

Even today, few offenders, other than those pleading guilty to minor street offences such as prostitution or drunkenness, can expect to know their fate within 24 hours of their arrest. 'Having the case hanging over one's head' often for several weeks is a common feature of the present system and one which causes considerable anxiety to many defendants. Ironically, perhaps these delays are frequently the result of well-intentioned policy changes designed specifically to help defendants. In the first place, delays often occur between charging by the police and the defendant's first appearance before the magistrates. In the past most defendants used to be held overnight at the police station and brought before the court the following morning, that is within 24 hours of their arrest. Today, however, the police seem far more willing to release defendants on bail to appear in court several days or even two or three weeks after being charged. A second indirect cause of delays is the increased availability of legal aid and the desire of many including some magistrates and clerks to see defendants represented by lawyers. Despite a notice on the back of the charge sheet used by many police stations advising defendants of the existence of legal aid, many defendants still appear at the first hearing unrepresented, only to be told by the magistrate or clerk that they should seek a lawyer's help before deciding upon their plea or before sentence is passed. Even those defendants who go to a solicitor's office before they are due to appear in court often do so only a day or so before the first hearing, so that in all but the most simple and straightforward cases the solicitor will almost inevitably request an adjournment in order to prepare the defence or plea in mitigation.

The surest way for a defendant to minimise delays at the magistrates' court is to plead guilty[13] for a plea of not guilty inevitably brings prosecution and defence to their feet to request an adjournment. Moreover, contested cases are invariably given low priority at magistrates' courts which, in busy courts, means that the defendant may well have to wait several months before his case is tried. Yet even a guilty plea does not absolutely guarantee a swift disposal of the case. As the Sheffield study indicates, many guilty pleaders were still subjected to adjournments and delays, although a proportion of cases adjourned at the request of prosecution or defence was considerably less than for not guilty pleas.[14] Rather these delays are more likely to be the result of the magistrate's calling for social enquiry reports. The attempt by magistrates to individualise sentences so as to meet the needs of particular defendants has therefore resulted in yet further delays even after the plea of guilty has been taken. These reports have to be prepared by a probation officer, which usually take three or four weeks.

Although it is difficult to predict with any accuracy how long a defendant will have to wait between charging by the police and sentence, it would not be unusual for a represented guilty pleader on whom the magistrates require a social enquiry report to wait six weeks to two months for the final sentence. On the other hand, a few are fortunate enough to leave court after the first hearing with their case completed.

Defendants tend to complain bitterly about the delays they experience in the criminal justice process. Some even attribute their guilty pleas to a desire to 'get it all over and done with'.[15] Indeed, there is no doubt that the inconvenience and anxiety caused to defendants through long delays and repeated court appearances features in the decision of many defendants to plead guilty rather than contest the case against them. This does not necessarily mean that all defendants who claimed that they pleaded guilty to save themselves time and trouble are innocent, but it does imply that there may well be some innocent defendants who either persuade themselves or are persuaded by others that the trouble and anxiety of contesting the case outweigh the possibility of an eventual acquittal.[16]

Finally, it should not be assumed that delays are always bad for defendants. Indeed, provided he is on bail rather than in custody, the long period between being charged and sentenced may allow a defendant to 'clean up his image' so that when his lawyer eventually presents him to the magistrates for sentencing, he may have found himself a job or a permanent place to live. Both these factors may be instrumental in obtaining for him a more lenient sentence than he might otherwise have received had the hearing taken place within 24 hours of his arrest.

3. Being Represented by a Lawyer under Legal Aid

Although help for a defendant in the context of magistrates' court hearings may include support from friends, relations and employers willing to stand by him and even act as his bail surety, for our purposes help means advice on how to plead and assistance in dealing with the complexities of the legal process. Earlier, we have seen how policemen sometimes advise defendants to plead guilty. Their advice may on occasions also extend to predicting for the defendant what sort of sentence he might expect, telling him what to say to the magistrates and informing him on how to conduct himself in court and even recommending a solicitor. Moreover, it would be a mistake to believe that a police officer's help is always inspired by self-interest. There are many instances where police officers feel sympathy for defendants and genuinely wish to assist them. Furthermore, once a defendant has confessed and agreed to plead guilty, it is generally of little importance to the officers concerned with the case what sort of sentence he receives.

Over the past twelve years an increasing proportion of defendants in magistrates' courts have turned to lawyers for help. Many of them, when they see a solicitor for the first time, believe themselves to be guilty. What help then do they expect from their lawyer? The answer varies from defendant to defendant. Some foster the hope, not altogether unfounded, that common-sense guilt may be somewhat different from legal guilt and that it may still be possible to avoid a conviction. Others may be charged with several offences arising from the same incident. In such cases the defendant may foresee some chance of his lawyer negotiating with the police for some charges to be dropped in return for guilty pleas in others. Yet, almost all intending guilty pleaders go to a solicitor above all in order to minimise the intervention of the court in his life.

Why a defendant chooses a particular solicitor for help is often a matter of chance rather than design. Those who prior experience of a particular solicitor, even if it was only in relation to the purchase of their home, will often contact him, at least in the first instance. Defendants who have not previously had any contact with a solicitor, may rely on recommendations from friends, relations, co-defenders, cellmates or even the police. A number of organisations, such as Release, the National Council for Civil Liberties, community and minority advice groups and law centres also keep lists of solicitors in whom they have confidence. Yet a surprising number of defendants simply accept a solicitor assigned to them by the court through Duty Solicitor schemes or randomly pick out a name from the list of local legal aid lawyers supplied by the court. Some simply walk into the first solicitor's office they happen to pass.[17]

Most defendants in magistrates' courts simply cannot afford the full cost of hiring a lawyer to appear in court on their behalf. The criminal legal aid system allows them to instruct a lawyer, generally of their choice, in the knowledge that, although they may be asked to contribute towards his fees, the bulk of the cost will usually be borne by the legal aid fund. This fund has, therefore, become an increasing source of income for lawyers practising in the criminal courts and, as a consequence, the criminal legal aid system has developed into an increasingly important structural factor influencing the nature of the lawyer-client relationship in magistrates' court.

Solicitors' firms are businesses. They depend for their existence on the profits gained from the services they give to the public. Clients, all clients that is, represent the firm's business assets. It is through them that overheads are covered and profits made. But where the legal aid client differs from the paying client is in the fact that, rather than being himself a source of the lawyer's income, he merely provides the lawyer with the keys to the coffers of public funds. It is through him rather than by him that the lawyer's bill is paid. The existence of the legal aid system, therefore, divorces the service from the payment. It is true that many defendants are required to pay contributions towards their legal aid costs. As this contribution does not find its way into the solicitor's pocket, rather it goes via the court to the legal aid fund; solicitors or the barristers they brief, do not, therefore, depend upon clients for their fees, as these are met direct from the legal aid fund whether or not the client actually pays his contribution. Under this system, neither the client's wealth nor his trustworthiness have any relevance for the lawyer. The only important matter is that he should qualify for legal aid. Defendants may become, in effect, a commodity to be sought after and accumulated. It is not unusual to hear solicitors coming back from court boast to their colleagues how many clients they 'picked up' that morning. Bankowski and Mungham write in their study of the Cardiff Duty Solicitor Scheme that:

> Many of the solicitors we talked to had firm ideas of what constituted a 'good case' to handle. The good case was never simply the case that had held some special legal interest (unlike the medical profession, where the good case is almost always seen as the clinically interesting one), or even one that was financially profitable in its own terms. Instead, the good case was the one that might conceivably lead on to a bonanza.[18]

The basis for payment of solicitors under criminal legal aid is simply one of time. The solicitor states in his bill how long he has spent taking statements and attending court and then proposes what he considers to be an adequate remuneration for his work. It is then up to the Legal Aid Area Authority to decide whether the rate of remuneration is reasonable and whether the time spent in preparation of the case was really necessary. Except in so far as some of the solicitor's file papers are sent to the Area Secretary's Office, there is no attempt to relate the amount of the lawyer's fee to the quality of the service he provides. The system thus makes it quite possible for the inefficient, uncaring lawyer, who is only concerned with the rapid turnover of business, to receive the same remuneration as the conscientious, efficient lawyer. Worse still, a solicitor who spares no effort in the services of his client may very well suffer if the extra work he puts into a case or the expenses he incurs are considered unnecessary by the Legal Aid Authority.

This is not to suggest that the clients themselves are bursting with complaints about their lawyers. The only methodical consumer studies of lawyers' services in the criminal courts suggest that the opposite is true.[19] Moreover, solicitors tended to be judged much more favourably than barristers.[20] Yet these studies in fact tell one little about the actual quality of legal services provided. Defendants, particularly those appearing in the lower courts, often have little or no prior experience of the criminal justice system and therefore no criteria by which to judge their lawyer's performance. Furthermore, satisfaction is notoriously manipulable; it may, for example, simply be a measure of the extent to which the client's expectations concerning the outcome of his case are fulfilled and the lawyer may play a large part in creating those expectations whether or not he plays a large part in their fulfilment.

A legally aided client who is dissatisfied with the service he is receiving from the solicitor and wishes to withdraw his instructions is faced with the problem that only the court which has granted the legal aid order is able to transfer that order to another solicitor. Magistrates' clerks vary in their attitude towards applications to transfer orders, but many of them insist on being provided with very good reasons for the change of solicitor and in at least one London stipendiary court they appeared to operate a policy that only in exceptional cases should such transfers be permitted. This is not to suggest that all lawyers working in magistrates' courts and representing defendants under legal aid are uncaring rogues intent on making as much money as possible at the expense of their clients — far from it, there are many solicitors and barristers who provide an excellent service for their clients. The point is that the legal aid system is to an important degree reliant upon the integrity, conscientiousness and self-monitoring of lawyers and in the case of some lawyers this reliance is sadly misplaced. Moreover, as with the police, it would be a mistake to lay the blame for every failing in the system at the feet of a few deviants. There are rather structural factors which make it both possible and expedient for lawyers to use the system to promote their own interests. The lawyer-client relationship is an example of this phenomenon.

In textbook discussions of the lawyer's role in the courts the assumption almost always is that that relationship between lawyer and client is a one-to-one affair, with the lawyer who first interviews the client going on to act for him throughout the course of his trial. This assumption is shared by many who know nothing about the actual operation of solicitors' offices. In reality the situation is often very different. Even in small provincial solicitors' firms it is not unusual to find interviews being conducted by legal executives or articled clerks and not by the solicitor who eventually appears for the defendant in court. This means the client will often meet a solicitor only on the morning of the court hearing. Moreover, in the London area, the shortage of solicitors available to carry out an ever increasing amount of work in the magistrates' courts has meant that barristers have appeared there more and more frequently. The rules governing the division of labour in the legal profession dictate that the lay person may only approach the barrister through the medium of a solicitor. Thus, the member of the solicitor's firm who interviews the client will normally send a brief to the barrister, setting out the facts and legal issues together with statements from the client and witnesses. Here again, the first contact between defendant and advocate will usually not take place until the morning of the hearing. At best this division of labour results in the defendant having to relate to two or more lawyers during the course of his progress through the criminal justice system. It also means that in many cases he is obliged to put his fate into the hands of someone he has met only a few minutes previously and in whom he is unlikely to have established any real confidence.

At worst this lack of continuity may provide an excuse for the solicitor's firm to take only scant instructions and carry out no preparation at all of the case. Some London barristers complain of solicitors whose briefs contain no more than the client's name and the offence with which he had been charged. There is even a lawyer's joke about solicitors for whom preparing a brief means no more than 'tying a piece of red ribbon around the client and sending him along to meet counsel at court'. Instructions in such cases are taken by the barrister who makes a few hurried notes in the courtroom corridor or cells while waiting for the case to be called. Matters are made worse by the fact that magistrates' courts tend to be training grounds for young, inexperienced barristers[21] Moreover, because of the way in which many barristers' chambers operate, there is no guarantee that, if the case is adjourned for a further hearing the same barrister will be free to represent the defendant at the next court appearance. The ideal, therefore, of a close lawyer-client relationship in which the lawyer acts as guide, helper and strategist is often far removed from the reality of the situation.

Another illusion which tends quickly to be shattered by harsh reality concerns the amount of time a solicitor is able or willing to spend on a particular client's case. First-time defendants in particular expect a personal, concerned service from their lawyer. For a solicitor, on the other hand, time is a commodity of his trade, which he uses in ways which are calculated to achieve the objective he seeks for himself and his practice. The failure of some solicitor firms to provide an adequate service to their clients in magistrates' courts usually arises from a policy of maximising profits by maintaining a low level of staffing and a high turnover of work. With each member of the firm carrying heavy case-loads, it is not surprising that only a limited amount of time can be allocated to each individual client. To be fair, many solicitors claim that the remuneration they receive from legal aid cases is so low that it prevents them from offering a first-class service. Yet, as with police officers' conduct towards suspects behind the closed doors of police stations, the norms that become established in practice in solicitors' offices are yet further examples of the way in which practices, however laudable, which hinder the achievement of private interests tend to fall into disuse and are replaced by other less desirable practices which help to attain these objectives. Thus, certain practices become established and institutionalised in solicitors' firms, such as interviews being scheduled every fifteen minutes, briefs being delivered to counsel at the last minute, pleas in mitigation being based on a few scant notes or upon the probation officer's social enquiry report rather than the solicitor's own enquiries, while other practices fall by the wayside, such as keeping clients informed on the progress of their case or advising them on their right of appeal after the hearing. These practices allow the lawyer to save himself time and effort in his work, but are clearly contrary to the client's best interests. Most clients, however, are not in a position to exercise any control over the quality of the service they receive, so that, in the absence of controls from other sources, the lawyer's performance passes off without criticism or complaint and his costs are paid without a murmur from the Legal Aid Fund.

Matters are, of course, made worse when a lawyer has a number of clients to represent in court on the same morning and it is particularly unsatisfactory when he has no contact with any of them until that morning. This is sometimes the position of Duty Solicitors who are expected to compress into the hour or so between their arrival at court and their first case all the preparation which, under ideal circumstances, would take twice or three times that amount of time.[22] Duty Solicitor schemes now operate in over 125 magistrates' courts. Their main purpose is to provide advice and representation for defendants who, for one reason or another, do not have a lawyer of their own in court. Usually a panel of local solicitors take it in turn to act as Duty Solicitor. The defendants are referred to them by the court and, after taking the client's instructions at the court, and representing him on that day, they usually continue to act for him as his solicitor. Major problems, however, arise where the Duty Solicitor is required to represent a defendant immediately without the benefit of adjournment to a future hearing date. This may occur when the defendant is in custody and wishes to contest a police application for bail or where he insists on having the case heard that day, which will involve the solicitor in making an almost impromptu plea in mitigation.

Such structural forces as pressure of time and the nature of the role they are obliged to play necessarily affects the way in which lawyers perceive and relate to their clients. Just as police perceptions of suspects are subject to stereotyping, so lawyers are influenced by such factors as the age, race, social class, dress and manner of their client. Bankowski and Mungham observe in their discussion of Cardiff Duty Solicitors that:

> There was an interest in helping, but some solicitors in this group made it clear that not everyone deserved their help. They operated like so many other counsellors of personal welfare with certain well defined stereotypes of 'deserving cases'. These were the contrite, humble, the grateful; especially favoured here were shoplifters, first time offenders, particularly women — with some honourable mention given to 'little old ladies', 'nice young ladies who really shouldn't have been in court at all', and the 'confused'. In these instances the solicitor clearly felt that a worthwhile job was being done. Other kinds of defendants, however, could expect a less welcoming and comfortable passage.[23]

Differences in class, culture or race between lawyers and clients may also be important. They may, for example, give rise to suspicion and mistrust. A common device used by lawyers who are unsympathetic to a particular client is to keep that client very much at arm's length, concealing his true feelings about the defendant and his defence behind a facade of formality and professionalism. Moreover, the stigma which attaches to the guilty in criminal cases, combined with the professional ethos of 'not becoming too involved', often result in lawyers developing techniques for distancing themselves from their clients both inside and outside the courtroom. It may also result in lawyers evolving a somewhat cynical attitude which may reveal itself in their discussions with other lawyers about their respective clients.

With few exceptions the position of magistrates' court defendants in relation to their lawyers is one of subservience and dependency. Most defendants are ignorant of the law, court procedures or of the norms of explicit and implicit bargaining that characterise much of the criminal justice process. Instead of instructing their lawyer what they want said or done, they are only too willing to abdicate from any responsibility for the conduct of their case. 'You know best', 'I'll leave everything to you', or 'You do what you think best, you are the expert' are common enough phrases in the ears of solicitors and barristers in offices, chambers and courtroom corridors. Moreover, it has to be remembered that most transactions between lawyers and inexperienced defendants take place while the defendant is in a state of heightened anxiety, which to some extent, lawyers are able to relieve by assuring their clients about the likely outcome of their case. 'If I plead guilty will they keep me in?' was the question that one researcher was most often asked when she carried out her research in the waiting rooms of magistrates' courts.[24] 'Have I got any chance of getting off?', 'What am I likely to get?', 'Will they send me down?' are questions which defence lawyers are continually being asked. Moreover, given the anxiety caused by the uncertainty and unfamiliarity of the situation and the fear of the court's penalty, most defendants are hardly in a position to criticise their lawyer, complain about the way he is conducting the case or attempt to seize control over its preparation and presentation in court.

4. Favours, Negotiations and Bargains

Whereas clients come and go, defence lawyers belong to a network of courtroom professionals and in many instances appear almost every day of the working week with the same prosecuting policemen or solicitors, the same police officers, the same clerks and the same station officers. The establishment and maintenance of good relationships between these regular participants is often based upon the exchange of small favours. These favours usually relate to arrangements for the hearing. The prosecutor, for example, might bring forward cases so as not to keep a defence lawyer waiting around the court. A probation officer may telephone a solicitor and disclose the recommendation he intends to make in his social enquiry report. A policeman may agree to the defence lawyer's suggestion that he inform the magistrates that the defendant was 'co-operative'. A defence lawyer may 'forget' to complain to the magistrates about police irregularities in preventing the client from contacting a lawyer. Generally, there is an unwritten rule amongst these regular participants not to embarrass, upset or unduly inconvenience one another in the staging of courtroom hearing. Similarly, good relations frequently depend on the participants avoiding conflict by 'not taking things too seriously'. Evidence of joking relationships, particularly between policemen, lawyers and clerks, may often be seen in the humorous exchanges that go on before the court opens or between sessions. Often one hears policemen and lawyers make remarks like 'It's only a game anyway.' Life, after all, would be terrible if the courtroom professionals allowed each issue where their interests conflicted to become a matter of major confrontation. Many of them openly admit that they prefer 'a quiet life' and the participant who is determined to fight tooth and nail threatens the delicate balance based on goodwill and a willingness to compromise. 'Fighters' soon earn themselves a reputation, as do participants who go back on their word. They become the courtroom deviants, not to be trusted and not worthy of favours.

Doing and receiving favours is very different from 'hard' bargaining. Bargaining in magistrates' courts takes place between parties who have specific 'commodities' that they are willing to exchange in return for a 'commodity' from the other side. These 'commodities' may include the power to offer no evidence on certain charges and this may be exchanged for a plea of not guilty, which represents the defendant's power to force the prosecution to prove the case.[25] This is the most common, but by no means the only type of bargain. In one recent case at Coventry magistrates' court in which I was involved, for example, the prosecution agreed to withdraw the charge of assaulting a policeman in return for the defendant dropping his official complaint against the policeman he was supposed to have assaulted. Information about stolen property or accomplices may also be an important 'commodity' in the hands of the defendant which the police may be prepared to buy with offers of reduced charges or release on bail.

Bargaining between defendants and police generally takes place at police stations before any charges have been brought. Often it concerns the police power to release defendants on bail or hold them in custody for several days. Police bail may and often is exchanged for a confession from the suspect. Experienced defendants may be able to win other concessions, while naive ones may throw away their bargaining position in response to phoney police threats.[26] As in most other forms of bargaining, bluff and counterbluff may be and often are employed by the more skilled players. Also, as in other forms of bargaining, the presence of an experienced intermediary may be crucial to the success of the deal. At police stations suspects usually have to bargain alone from a position of weakness and ignorance. At the court, on the other hand, the defence lawyer may well play this role of the intermediary and win important concessions from the prosecution — concessions which an inexperienced defendant on his own would never have thought possible. As well as charges being dropped, objections to bail sometimes evaporate and the estimated value of stolen property or illicit drugs may be reduced. Sometimes these concessions may be won without any apparent 'commodity' being surrendered by the defence. The reason is that it may be sufficient for the police officer in charge of the case or the prosecuting solicitor merely to know that the arguments they had intended to put to the court will be challenged by a fellow courtroom professional for some compromise to be reached and open conflict consequently avoided.

5. Being the Subject of a Social Enquiry Report

Turning now to the role of the probation officer in the sentencing process, it should first be emphasised that it is only in the minority of cases that the probation officer's services are required. Obviously, where the defendant is already on probation, his supervising officer will provide the court with an account of his progress or lack of progress during the period of supervision. More often, however, probation officers are called upon by the court to prepare a social enquiry report on a defendant with whom they have had no prior contact. Ideally, the social enquiry report is an 'objective appraisal of the offender and his circumstances designed to assist the court in determining the "most suitable method" of dealing with the offender'.[27] According to the Streatfield Report,[28] it should include 'among other things essential details of the offender's home surroundings, and family background; his attitude to the present offence; his attitude and response to previous forms of treatment following any previous convictions; detailed histories about relevant physical and mental conditions; and assessment of personality and character'. However, as so often in the criminal courts, there is a wide gap between ideal and practice. An analysis by Perry of the contents of 600 social enquiry reports found that 'the average report would be the length of one A4 page'. It would contain:

No statement about receipt of police antecedents
no mention of the amount of contact on which the report was based
no mention of living conditions
no description of the neighbourhood
no mention of financial position

no mention of the subject's leisure interests and associates

no mention of his religious or moral values

no mention of his health record

no identification of special problems

no assessment of subject's personality or potential

no mention of his life style; self-image; or interpretation of past, present or future

no interpretation of criminal record

no mention of police account of the offence

no mention of the fact of previous sentencing

no assessment of his attitude to the offence

no mention of the risk of further delinquency

only a mention of the members of his present household

some facts about his education/work record

a mention of the subject's account of the offence, but no comment on it

a recommendation

the basic facts regarding parents and siblings with either a statement about or an assessment of relationships.[29]

This and another recent study[30] indicate, moreover, that there is considerable variation in the content of social enquiry reports, depending upon the information available and the extent to which the probation officer concerned perceives meeting the needs of the defendant and those of the court as important objectives for the report. There is evidence that probation officers sometimes deliberately exclude unfavourable information, such as knowledge that the defendant 'had done a few jobs for which he had not been caught' or full details of the defendant's employment record where this would be 'too damaging to the recommendation'.[31] Furthermore, much more of the information contained in the report is likely to be favourable to the defendant than unfavourable.[32]

The extent to which probation officers attempt to verify information also varies considerably. Perry found that in over half the reports in his sample the officer based his information on only one interview with the defendant and only in slightly over half did he visit the home.[33] He also found that there was a tendency to rely on information obtained either direct from the defendant or from existing files.[34] Moreover, probation officers are liable to subject defendants to the same process of stereotyping and classification as policemen and lawyers, the only difference being that in general the probation officer's experience and training have provided him with more categories and more sophisticated categories into which defendants may be slotted. Nevertheless, the individual probation officer's response to the defendant at a personal level may still play an important part in determining what goes into his social enquiry report. Perry reports how he 'heard officers admit that someone who is aggressive or disrespectful in interview is less likely to be recommended for supervision than a subject who is pleasant and cooperative . . .' 'People working under pressure', he explains, 'are less likely to take on difficult and demanding cases, although they may be at least as needy as the ones they select.'[35]

The reaction of the probation officer to the defendant may also reveal itself in less obvious ways than in the recommendation for or against supervision. The same author states that it seems that 'the assessment of the subject's attitude toward authority was made during the interview . . . It seems to follow that very often when an officer was talking about a subject's attitude to authority he was meaning the attitude he had perceived the subject to be adopting to him.'[36] Thus both the information which the probation officer selects for presentation to the court and his interpretation of that information may depend in part upon his response to the way in which the defendant presented himself at the interview. Just as the more experienced probation officers may be more successful than novices in classifying defendants and in making acceptable recommendations, so the more experienced and perceptive defendants may learn to define themselves in terms of their social and personal problems in order to win the support of the probation officer.

The other major influence upon the contents of the probation officer's report and its recommendation is the court itself. Probation officers are dependent upon the confidence the magistrates have in their judgement if they are to wield any influence over sentencing. Therefore, if they go too far in the direction of leniency, they run the risk of being regarded by the bench as 'gullible' or 'soft' and thus not to be taken seriously. Leaning too far in the other direction, however, may conflict with their ideology as helpers and solvers of people's social problems. It is not surprising therefore that probation officers in preparing their reports take into account the various idiosyncracies of different courts and individual magistrates.[37] One author has described the relationship between probation officers and magistrates as a 'closed loop system' with the probation officer perceiving from the magistrate's past reactions to his recommendations the likely response to any recommendations he may make in the future. Accordingly, this knowledge will influence his recommendation which, in turn, will reinforce the magistrate's opinion of the reliability and expertise of the probation officer.[38] Perry gives some empirical support for the existence of such a 'closed loop system' in his finding that the more experienced the probation officer, the more his recommendations 'come into line' with the actual proportions of the court's sentencing at least in so far as the recommendations of a probation order were concerned.[39]

Once the probation officer has selected what he considers to be relevant information for the court and has decided upon his recommendation, it is extremely difficult for either the defendant or his lawyer to challenge the probation officer's judgement. For instance, the normal controls over the acceptability and presentation of evidence which apply before conviction, such as the hearsay rule and cross-examination, are relaxed as soon as the defendant is found guilty.[40] Although the defendant or his solicitor may request the personal attendance in court of the probation officer who prepared the social enquiry report, in practice this rarely happens — often because it involves delays which the defendant will wish to avoid.[41] The usual procedure is that the defendant or his lawyer does not receive a copy of the report until the morning of the hearing. When the case is called, a probation officer, not necessarily the one who prepared the report, will present copies to the magistrates and after they have read the reports, the defendant or his lawyer will be asked if they have anything to say in mitigation. Only rarely will the officer who was actually responsible for the report be required to go into the witness box and be subjected to questions from the defendant or his lawyer about its contents. On the occasions when this does happen, it usually is extremely difficult for the defendant or his lawyer to challenge the contents of the report or the recommendation without giving the impression that is the probation officer's judgement or integrity that is being attacked. To give such an impression is not only disruptive to the network of courtroom regulars but is also likely to prove counter-productive, as generally the magistrates and the clerk of the court will protect the probation officer against any attempt to undermine his authority.

It is difficult to establish with any certainty the amount of influence social enquiry reports actually have on individual sentences, since the report may be one of several sources of information and influence affecting the sentencing decision. In addition, the degree of complexity of different variables makes meaningful comparisons between defendants who were the subject of social enquiry reports and those who were not a difficult, if not impossible exercise. However, a controlled simulated study on 175 magistrates using genuine social enquiry reports from previous cases found that the information provided by probation officers did appear to influence magistrates' sentencing decisions in the direction of the sentence which the probation officer felt to be appropriate. Furthermore, this information combined with a formal recommendation proved more influential than information alone.[42] In another experiment it was found that among all the information that was likely to be contained in a social enquiry report, the three categories which magistrates considered most important for their sentencing decision were details of the offence, previous convictions and the defendant's attitude to the offence.[43] The first two of these three categories are in any event always presented to the magistrates in the police antecedents and the third is often available in the police 'brief facts' or the defendant's confession to the police.

Finally, it should not be imagined, however, that the relationship between probation officers and the court is invariably one of mutual respect and co-operation. There are, for example, occasions when there can be no effective compromise between the conflicting roles of the probation officer as agent of the court and social worker. Moreover, sometimes he finds himself caught in the crossfire between his client and the court with the result that his relationship with one or the other is bound to be damaged. The following extract from a social enquiry report concerning a 17-year-old girl illustrates this point:

> This period since the hearing — — 19 — has been a particularly difficult one in terms of my involvement with B. She remains extremely bitter at being found guilty and continues to plead her innocence. I had hoped that the deferred sentence would have aided my attempt to seek the cooperation of B in planning for the future of her other daughter, J, who is in the care of the local authority at present. However, the reverse has been true. B's attitude towards authority has hardened since the hearing and there has been a deterioration of her willingness to cooperate with me from that date.

6. At the Court

There are almost 700 magistrates' court buildings in England and Wales and many of them contain two or more courtrooms. The majority of these buildings were purpose-built in the early part of this century.

Thus, the image conjured up by the words 'magistrates' court' tends to be of a rather austere, red-bricked edifice with large, arched doorways and windows. Inside, there are usually several passageways with doors leading off them to the individual courtrooms, the clerk's office and the magistrates' retiring rooms. At the end of one of the passageways there is a heavy door with either a spy-hole or an iron grill. This is the entrance to the cells and is manned by a police officer who unlocks the door for lawyers and probation officers wishing to make last-minute visits to those of their clients being held in custody. Until about five years ago all defendants who had been released on bail by police or magistrates were obliged formally to surrender to bail and were taken down to the cell area to await their case. Today, however, few courts continue this practice. Instead, defendants are simply required to inform the warrant officer or usher that they are present and they may then remain in the courtroom corridor or waiting area until their case is called. A visitor to any busy magistrates' court in the mid-morning of any weekday will find a crowd of people milling around the entrance to each court — defendants, lawyers, policemen, witnesses, sureties — some sitting, some standing, some scribbling hurried notes or reading through documents, some squeezing past one another to get into and out of the court.

Although there is no uniform courtroom design, most of them follow a general pattern.[44] Number one court at Coventry, illustrated in Figure 2 has all the typical features. The courtroom is divided into three main areas which correspond roughly to the three different functions of those present, the judges, the judged and the spectators. The 'judges' are the magistrates and court clerks who operate from one end of the courtroom. The magistrates enter and leave the courtroom through their own door, which the clerks also use when they go to assist the magistrates on points of law. The magistrates' seats are symbolically raised above everyone else in the courtroom and above them is the royal emblem of lion and unicorn. In the well of the court are all those professional participants involved in specific cases; they are seeking, awaiting or trying to influence the decisions of the magistrates and include lawyers, policemen and probation officers. At the far end of the courtroom to the magistrates are the public benches, which are used by sureties, character witnesses and friends and relations of the defendants as well as by disinterested spectators. Members of the press are treated, geographically, at least, as professionals rather than spectators, being provided with special seats in the well of the court.

The dock, like the magistrates' bench, is usually raised above floor

Figure 2: Sketch Plan of Coventry City Magistrates' Court, No. 1 Court

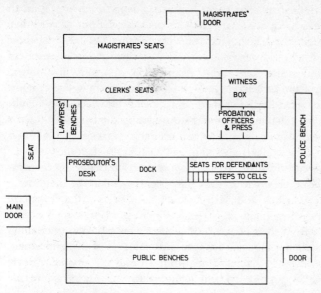

level. Often it is positioned, as in Coventry number one court, in the centre of the court, but in some courtrooms it is situated behind the lawyers' benches. The dock itself is a square, wooden construction with a partition topped by an iron rail on three of its sides. The fourth side is open and leads down some steps to the cell area. Although practices vary from court to court, by no means all defendants are confined to the dock during their case. Those who appear on summonses, for example, often stand and sit directly in front of the dock rather than in it. However, whether they are in front of the dock or inside it, communications between defendants and anyone else in the courtroom necessarily take place across much greater distances than is normal for face-to-face conversational exchanges. Indeed, it is unlikely that the average, first-time offender will previously have experienced a situation where he has to stand up and address people several yards away except perhaps in the school classroom or public meetings. In fact the task facing defendants is often more difficult than that facing speakers at public meetings, for the defendants frequently have to respond to questions by addressing someone other than the questioner. In sentencing hearings, for example, the clerk may ask the questions, but answers should be directed at the magistrates.[45]

Even communications between the defendant and his own lawyer may prove extremely difficult in the courtroom, for the dock is often to the side of or some distance behind the lawyers' benches. It must be remembered that most magistrates' courts were built at a time when few defendants had lawyers to represent them. Yet, even in those courts constructed during the last ten years, the design of the courtroom gives no assistance to defendants wishing to consult with their lawyers during their case. Indeed, it is extremely rare in any magistrates' court to see a defendant initiate contact with his own lawyer. Occasionally they do so by catching the lawyer's eye, asking the magistrates for a short adjournment or passing written or oral messages via court ushers or warrant officers, but, usually, any such contact is the result of initiatives either from the defence lawyer or from the bench or clerk. The only occasion when it commonly occurs is when the magistrates have imposed a fine and wish to know at what rate the defendant wishes to pay instalments. The general reluctance of lawyers to take instructions from their clients during the course of court proceedings is understandable, for it means that everything must come to a halt, after which there is a long silence while all eyes rest upon the dock, where lawyer and client converse in loud whispers, only too aware that everyone in the courtroom can hear what they are saying.

Not all magistrates' court hearings take place in purpose-designed courtrooms. In Coventry, as at many other courts, there are several ordinary rooms containing simple tables and chairs, which are used as courtrooms. Yet, as far as possible, the furniture in these rooms is arranged in imitation of the formal courtroom, with the defendant's chair being isolated from the others. The same is true of court hearings which take place in buildings other than courthouses, such as town halls. Thus, even where the opportunity exists to reduce the physical and psychological distance between the defendant and other courtroom participants or to organise the court so that the defendant sits next to his lawyer, the formal, traditional layout is invariably preferred.

7. Being Sentenced

The prevailing assumption which determines to a considerable degree the nature of the sentencing hearing is that court's sentence is the result of a process of rational assessment of all available information concerning the offender and the offence.[46] Clearly, there are limits upon lengths to which the court is prepared to go in its attempt to discover information about the defendants and these limits vary from case to case and from court to court. As a general rule, sentences for minor transgressions such as drunkenness and disorderly behaviour are based upon very little information. Usually, the clerk will open the proceedings by asking the defendant his name, age and address. Then the prosecutor (policeman or solicitor) or the police officer in charge of the case will describe the circumstances of the offence in a sentence or two, offer a brief summary of the defendant's record, and read out any confession that the prisoner may have made to the police. Apart from asking the defendant if he has anything to say, the magistrates will generally not attempt to seek any further information before sentencing him to a small fine or, in the case of a repeating offender, to a short spell in prison. For more serious crimes the court will often take more trouble to find out details of the offence and full background information about the offender. Frequently, however, policemen, prosecuting solicitors and defence lawyers will anticipate the magistrate's requirements and provide them unprompted with such information. Yet, it should not be imagined that the perceived seriousness of the offence is necessarily the only or even the major factor in determining the extent of the court's demand for information. The atypicality of the offence may be as important as its seriousness. An offender, for example, who assaults a police officer during a street demonstration is likely to provoke fewer enquiries from the court than an offender who commits a similar offence when the police attempt to intervene in a domestic dispute at his home. The former offence is likely to be regarded as situationally typical in the sense that offences of this sort are regularly committed upon police victims in the context of street demonstrations, while the latter offence may well be perceived as unusual or irregular.[47]

Moreover, the defendant's characteristics, his age, his record and his 'normality' would also determine the extent of the court's informational requirements. The magistrates will, for example, almost invariably require a social enquiry report on any young offender on whom they anticipate imposing a custodial sentence. Yet they are also likely to request a report on a defendant guilty of a trivial offence, where his history or the circumstances of the offence put them on enquiry. An example might be that of an irrational shoplifter who accumulates a stock of stolen items which are of no apparent value to him. In general, women elicit more enquiries from the court than men, simply because female criminals are generally perceived as 'abnormal'.

The location of the court is also an important determinant of its information requirements. The magistrates at Marlborough Street Magistrates' Court in the West End of London spend much less time enquiring into the backgrounds of prostitutes and shoplifters than, for example, the magistrates at Coventry. One obvious reason for this difference is simply that the crowded court lists at Marlborough Street allow the magistrates much less time for the consideration of each individual case, but locational variations also reflect differences in attitude over what constitutes behaviour serious enough and abnormal enough to warrant further investigation. Moreover, the more problematic the case for sentencing purposes the more information the court is likely to require in the hope that their enquiries will reveal some clue that will assist them in determining the sentence.

The courtroom relationship between the defendant and the stipendiary magistrates or chairmen of lay benches and the court clerk varies considerably between different courts, depending on court traditions as well as the personalities of the magistrates and clerks. In some courts the chairman of the lay bench appears to have virtually no speaking part, while in others it is the clerk who remains silent while the chairman or stipendiary questions the defendant and explains to him the meaning of the court's decisions. Courts also vary in the degree to which they use the unrepresented defendant as a source of information about himself. Sometimes, only a token question is directed at him — 'Have you anything to say?' or 'What have you got to tell me?' The usual response to this approach is silence or a mumbled apology. At other times a court official will make a real attempt to draw out the defendant. For example, clerks at Sheffield Magistrates' Court are instructed that

> Tongue-tied defendants must always be encouraged to talk; the best way is often to put a series of short simple questions about job; marital status, etc., before 'Now what do you want to tell the magistrates about the offence?'[48]

Yet even where these tactics are employed, most defendants, isolated in the dock and subject to the gaze of the public, are ill-prepared and ill-equipped to present to the magistrates a portrait of themselves or their offence which seriously challenges that given by the police or prosecutor.

Moreover, extracting information from a defendant may be such a lengthy and tedious process that magistrates and clerks, faced with long lists, simply do not have the time for the task. A much more convenient expedient may be to 'put the case back' either for a full social enquiry report or for the probation officer or duty solicitor to 'have a word with the defendant' outside the courtroom and report back later the same morning. Where the defendant does speak out, he will often attempt to bring in matters which are irrelevant to the proceedings. A further possibility is that he will attempt to step outside the role of 'accused' and 'penitent' and turn the court against his accusers by alleging police brutality or misconduct during arrest or interrogation. He may also attempt to excuse his conduct in terms of situational factors which relieve him of responsibility, such as 'everyone does it', 'I just went along with the others' or 'I was too drunk to know what was happening'. Such attempts to redefine the nature of the courtroom hearing are usually forestalled by the court clerk or the chairman who will interrupt the defendant and explain to him the court's boundaries of relevance or the legal definition of moral responsibility. This latter point is well illustrated by Pat Carlen in her account of a dialogue which followed the entry of a guilty plea by a ticket collector, charged with stealing from London Transport (pocketing fares at the barrier):

Magistrate: What do you want to say?

Defendant: Well, it is something that can happen any time. Everybody does it. I didn't mean to do it.

Magistrate: Mr. Grant! You have pleaded guilty to four charges under the Theft Act which all involve intention. Do you wish to change your plea? Which is what you should do, if you now say that you had no intention.

Defendant: No, Sir.

Magistrate: This is sad, very sad. So tragic. Your whole character and job gone for this miserable little amount. One doesn't like to moralize but there is this attitude of anything goes.[49]

Where the defendant is legally represented, it is up to the defence lawyer to contribute to the information-gathering process and, at the same time, to attempt to persuade the court that their clients are lesser sinners than the facts of the case, as presented by the prosecution, suggest. First, the defence solicitor or barrister may ask the police officer, presenting the prosecution's 'facts', questions that may correct any misimpressions that he may have given to the court — 'It's right, isn't it, Officer, that Mr Smith never actually went into the building?'

— or bring out points in his client's favour — 'It's correct, is it not, Officer, that all the stolen property has now been recovered?' or 'Is it correct, Officer, that Mr Smith co-operated fully with the police after his arrest?'

Secondly, the defence lawyer may offer the court an explanation for his client's conduct which, while not challenging the court's concept of relevance and causality, nevertheless presents him in a sympathetic and favourable light. For example, wherever possible, defence lawyers will pursue an episodic rather than a dispositional interpretation of their client's behaviour, stating, for example, that the offence was 'quite out of character' and bringing evidence, such as a letter from an employer or youth club organiser to show normal, law-abiding behaviour in other situations. Where such episodic interpretations are not appropriate, they will typically offer an explanation in terms of their client's personal pathology, and at the same time will resist the suggestion that this pathology be defined as a moral failure. Rather than being 'evil', 'dishonest', 'aggressive' or 'exploitive' they prefer to describe their clients as 'immature', 'easily led', 'lacking in self-control', 'over-excitable' or 'subject to bouts of depression'.[50]

In the third place, there is the tactic of blaming someone who is not present in court for the defendant's involvement in crime. The alcoholic husband of a shoplifting wife may, according to the defence lawyer, be responsible for his wife's depressed condition and hence for the offence she has committed. Similarly, a wife's adultery may be identified as the cause of the defendant 'going to pieces' and turning to crime.

Fourthly, the defence lawyer may, through a process of selection and interpretation, present to the court the most favourable features of their client's background, history and present situation. Periods when the defendant was not actually arrested are, for example, typically interpreted as evidence that he was 'making an effort to stay out of trouble' or 'leading a good, honest life'. Similarly, periods with no convictions at a time when the defendant was under the supervision of a probation officer are likely to be interpreted as demonstrating that 'he is able to respond to the friendship and guidance which the probation service is able to offer'. Defence lawyers may also make good use of any social enquiry report by selecting and drawing to the attention of the magistrates those points which indicate that their client is worthy of help rather than deserving punishment according to the tariff.

Fifthly, defence lawyers may present the court with their client's apologies and repentance for the damage, loss or trouble he has caused, and where appropriate, make an offer of amends on his behalf. They may also attempt to win the sympathy of the bench by pointing out the various ways in which their client has already suffered as a result of his misconduct. He may, for example, have spent a period in custody awaiting trial, lost his job or 'been disgraced by having to appear before the magistrates' court'. Such pleas for sympathy are usually accompanied by assurances as to their client's future conduct. The court appearance or spell in prison is often described as having a 'therapeutic effect' or as being a 'watershed' or 'turning point' in his life. There is less need, in other words, to punish severly a defendant who has 'already learnt his lesson'.

Finally, many defence lawyers will attempt to pre-empt the magistrates' decision by suggesting possible ways of dealing with the defendant. Most are careful not to give the impression that they are telling the bench what to do and will use such tactful phrases as 'you might be minded to . . .' or 'you may be of the opinion that' to emphasise that the decision lies, of course, in the hands of the magistrates. They will often in defining the sentencing process use the language of problem-solving, with their client presenting a problem for which the court has to find a solution. In cases where the defendant has been in trouble several times before, for example, the lawyer will frequently appeal to the court for 'a last chance' before the ultimate sanction of prison. Here, the last chance is typically described as being a positive or constructive solution to the problem, while prison is always referred to in a negative way, a totally destructive answer to the problem, a recourse of despair rather than hope.

Magistrates are not generally required to give reasons for their sentencing decisions, and, in fact, rarely do so. More often than not they simply announce their sentence and leave it at that. They may, however, seize the opportunity to express their condemnation of the offence, lecture the defendant on his conduct, warn him about the effects of repeating such conduct in the future and advising him generally about his life. Such judicial sermons are usually referred to as 'homilies'. These homilies are sometimes used by the magistrates to prevent creating the impression that they condone or excuse the defendant's criminal behaviour. Thus, they appear to be much prevalent in cases where the magistrate's sentence might be interpreted as being on the lenient side.[51] One often hears a magistrate, when ordering a conditional discharge, for example, telling the defendant that he will take a serious view of his behaviour if that defendant appears before him again or, when the bench decides not to bring into effect a suspended sentence, warning the defendant that this is positively his last chance.

Magistrates' homilies may also include paternalistic exhortations or advice about the defendant's future conduct. Often such advice does little more than to reinforce the principle of law and courtroom morality that the defendant is a free agent entirely responsible for his behaviour. Thus magistrates may advise defendants to "get their job back', 'get themselves fixed up' or 'get another job'. Exhortations also follow this general principle of personal responsibility by impressing upon the defendant the importance of avoiding further trouble, making use of the opportunity the court has given him and not letting down his family or friends.

Yet, on some occasions magistrates will step outside their role and beyond the formal requirements of justice to make genuine offers of help to defendants who are presented as having immediate personal problems. A magistrate might, for instance, ask the probation officer to find a homeless defendant a place to live in a hostel or offer to pay his fare back to his parents' home out of the court fund. Similarly, a magistrate may refer an illiterate defendant to a literacy scheme or a lonely defendant to a social club.

The way in which magistrates arrive at their sentencing decision is a complete mystery to a majority of defendants. The most they see of the process is usually a brief exchange of whispers between the members of the lay bench, or a short pause for thought, in the case of a stipendiary magistrate. If there is any possible disagreement or if the chairman of the bench feels a proper discussion is needed, the magistrates will withdraw to their retiring room leaving the defendant to bite his nails, the clerk to get on with his paperwork and policemen and lawyers to discuss the weekend's golf or the price of houses.

Since researchers are not permitted to invade the privacy of the retiring room and since magistrates are unwilling to discuss the way in which they arrive at specific sentencing decisions, one may write only in very general terms about the decision-making process of magistrates. One important feature which Elizabeth Burney found from her interviews with magistrates is the comparative ease with which they appear to reach a consensus about the right way of dealing with an offender.[52] Burney sees this as a product in part of the selection process which tends 'to favour a "clubbable" type of person' and 'to eliminate people with obviously extreme opinions . . .'[53]

From the description given by those magistrates interviewed, she was able to identify three factors as being of prime importance in the process of decision-making. 'First and foremost was the pressure to fit in with the team, not to stand out too far too long so as to delay a decision unreasonably . . .' Secondly, was the deference new magistrates felt for their more experienced colleagues. Finally, was an acceptance of the chairman of the bench as a decision-leader with freedom to exercise his influence 'freely or with conscious restraint' according to the personality of the individual chairman.[54]

A study by Bond and Lemon on changes in the attitudes of new magistrates gives some support to the notion of a socialisation process by which magistrates gradually fall into line with the attitudes of existing members of the bench towards different types of offenders and different offences[55] However, except perhaps in the case of stipendiary magistrates, it would be wrong to attribute the socialisation process and the consequent variations in the policies of different courts solely to the influence of the personality and attitude of individuals. Roger Hood suggests rather that magistrates' courts should be viewed as more or less self-contained organisations, each one following its own tradition and restraints rather than being just a collection of people with individual views. The Home Office research study on sentencing discrepancies provides some support for this observation in its conclusion that 'courts were only really interested in maintaining consistency within their own practice', and, with the exception of fines for motoring offences, 'No court spokesman claimed that any attempt was made to achieve consistency with his neighbours.'[56]

Finally, the influence of the Clerk to the Justices on the magistrates' sentencing decisions may be much greater than is suggested by the official rules, which, as we have seen, permit only advice to magistrates when requested and then only on questions of law or mixed law and fact. The justices' clerk is involved in the training of new magistrates and is often responsible for disseminating information and guidance to members of the bench through bulletins, newsletters or circulars or by other less formal means. He is also responsible for scheduling business and drawing up the magistrates' rota. The author of the Home Office sentencing study called him a 'mediator of court traditions'.[57] Certainly his potential for influencing magistrates' attitudes is enormous, not only in his role outside the courtroom, but also as court clerk.

Despite the formal restrictions placed on the clerk's courtroom role, it is clear that in many courts he does advise on sentencing, even where strictly no questions of law arise. Some benches of magistrates may even call upon him and be grateful for his advice on decisions for

which they alone should be responsible. Burney records that in one of
the benches she studied the clerk was regularly used by the magistrates
to resolve differences of opinion between them.

> One court chairman . . . said that if his colleagues proposed a fine
> he thought too high 'I ring for the clerk and we talk it over and the
> advice of the clerk carries a lot of weight . . .'[58]

8. Having One's Name in the Paper

For many defendants, particularly those with unblemished records, a
far worse consequence of conviction by the magistrates than any
formal penalty which the court may impose is the possibility of 'the
papers getting hold of the story'. Even for the most minor cases this is
a very real possibility. Whether or not a case is reported depends to
a large extent on chance factors, such as the presence of a reporter in
court, the news-value of the case in the estimation of the reporter and
editor, the amount of space available in the paper. Chance factors
also play a part in determining in how much detail the matters revealed
in the courtroom find their way into print. In some cases it may be no
more than a name, an address and details of the sentence. At other
times, however, the newspaper report may seize upon some epithet or
some choice phrase used by the magistrate, police, defence lawyer or
the defendant himself and use it as a lead into the report. The reports
set out below contain a number of stories using this technique, such as
the one headed, 'Crash victim started row when nurse said "strip" ' —
a detail in this case which was totally irrelevant to the offences charged
— and the use of the words, 'in a temper', 'by mistake', and 'foolish'
in the headlines and their elaboration in the report itself. The fact
that these latter three reports relate to nothing more serious than
criminal damage and 'drink-driving' indicates the way in which local
newspapers use accounts of the most petty cases to fill their pages.
There is even a report of the names and addresses of seven defendants
who had failed to pay their television licence fees.

Court cases are, after all, easy game for newspapers. They need
send only a pair of junior reporters along to the local magistrates' court
for a morning's work and they may return to the office armed with a
dozen or more stories of human folly, evil and misery. For most defendants, the court reporter is an ogre sent to torment him. On many

From the Coventry *Evening Telegraph* September 5th 1979.

Teenager 'narrowly escaped jail'

7½-year driving ban for 'foolish' lad

AN 18-YEAR-OLD butcher has been banned from driving for 7½ years by Stratford - on - Avon magistrates.

And C K was told that he had narrowly escaped being sent to prison.

K was in court yesterday for sentence on 14 motoring offences, including two for drink-driving. His ban is thought to be the longest ever imposed by the court.

The presiding magistrate, Mr Philip Walker, told him:

"You showed complete disregard for the law and flouted the police.

"When you go out of this court, bear in mind that you are a very lucky man. We nearly sent you to prison and very well might have done had you not been planning to get married soon".

Skidded

K of Stratford, was fined £100 and banned for 12 months on each of two offences of driving with excess alcohol, the disqualifications to run concur-

rently. He was also ordered to pay £25·48 costs.

For the 12 other offences, he was disqualified for a total of 6½ years and put on probation for two years.

The offences included four counts of driving without insurance, four of driving without a licence, and one case each of driving without due care and attention, failing to give his name and address after an accident, failing to report an accident and failing to produce a test certificate.

The offences followed incidents on January 11, April 21, May 2 and May 3 this

year, said Sgt. Ian Smith, prosecuting.

On January 11, K car damaged a hedge and a fence when it skidded on snow at Long Marston. Challenged by a resident, he had given a false name and address, said Sgt. Smith.

On April 21, K was involved in a collision with another car at Alcester Road, Stratford, in which the occupants of the other car were injured.

Marry

Mr Peter Nichols, defending, said that K had "a thoroughly shocking record, particularly disturbing because it occurred over such a short period."

But his client had been only five years old when his father had disappeared. Nobody knew where he was today. This doubtless had some effect on his life.

K had a good job and was planning to marry this year. "For the couple to have a home of their own will have a settling effect on him."

K who was told to pay the fines and costs at the rate of £8 a week, admitted three previous motoring offence — in March and December, 1977 and in June, 1978, when he was disqualified from driving for six months.

"You have been very, very foolish," Mr Walker told him.

Two bailed

Two men accused of inflicting grievous bodily harm on Philip Patrick Michael McMullan in Coventry on May 6, were remanded on bail until September 24, by Coventry magistrates.

O M B '20) and J B (21) both of Coventry, deny the charge.

Warrant for man on robbery charges

COVENTRY magistrates issued a warrant for the arrest of a man who failed to appear in court on two robbery charges.

W M C (28), of Ardrossan, Ayrshire, should have appeared with G P C (25), of Bedworth, and J A P (28), of Coventry.

G and P were each bailed until September 11, P with conditions that he reports daily to the police and lives at his home during the bail period.

All three are accused of robbing Mr Andrew Richard Jones of 20p, a watch and a quantity of keys, and robbing Mr Thomas Gerrard O'Donoghue of £1.50, nine cigarettes and a pair of shoes.

G is also accused of robbing Mr Colin Andrew Brindley of a wallet containing £20.

The offences are alleged to have happened in Coventry on July 29.

BENEFIT FRAUD MAN FINED

A MAN now working for the National Coal Board was fined a total of £60 and ordered to repay £75 by Rugby magistrates yesterday for making false claims for unemployment benefit.

K L W (32), of Wolston, had been remanded for a social enquiry report after pleading guilty to three cases of claiming benefit when he was being paid by a tyre company. He asked for two other offences to be considered.

Matrimonial and financial difficulties were put forward as the reason for the offences.

W was fined £20 on each charge and was ordered to pay £75 compensation to the Department of Health and Social Security and a £10 advocate's fee.

KICKED IN DOOR 'BY MISTAKE'

A COVENTRY man, who kicked down someone's front door thinking it was his own, was fined £10 and ordered to pay £60 compensation by Coventry magistrates yesterday.

K C (27) a carpenter, of Radford, Coventry, pleaded guilty to damaging the front door of 63, Grangemouth Road. The offence took place on August 12.

Chief Insp. Colin Such prosecuting said that C was drunk at the time and could not find his own door. He had not been living in for very long.

C said that he had just returned from Germany, when the offence took place. "I just got the wrong door," he said.

Broke window

A 17-year-old girl who smashed a window and a vase at the Richmond Fellowship home in Davenport Road, Coventry, was conditionally discharged and ordered to pay £48.50 compensation by Coventry magistrates.

D R of Clitiger, Burnley, who was under psychiatric care,

'in a temper'

had run away after five days at the home, said Chief Inspector Colin Such. She was returned to the hostel by police.

Mr Michael Taberner, defending, said that D ran out of the deputy warden's room during an interview and, in a fit of temper, threw a vase through a plate glass window.

From the Coventry Evening Telegraph September 5th 1979.

Crash victim started row when nurse said 'strip'

A ROAD accident victim created a disturbance when nurses told him to take off his clothes.

S   W   (21), told police that he was only taken to Warwick Hospital because a "do-gooder" had called an ambulance after he fell off his motor bike in West Street, Warwick.

His only injury was a cut finger, Stratford - on - Avon magistrates heard yesterday — and he didn't see why he had to get undressed for that.

He created a disturbance and was asked to leave, said Inspector Paul Tallett, prosecuting. Minutes later staff heard breaking glass and discovered that a reception room window had been smashed by W   's crash helmet.

W   unemployed, of Stratford, admitted driving carelessly, failing to give a blood or urine sample, and damaging the hospital window worth £31.61.

Stealing

He also admitted stealing £1,500 belonging to Ballater Caterers Ltd., stealing a Barclaycard and three cheques worth 25p and obtaining petrol by deception. He asked for 15 further offences to be considered.

W   M   D   (19), and S   D   C   (19), both of Stratford, also admitted entering 74a, Albany Road, Stratford, as trespassers on August 27 and stealing a TV, radio, worth £126, and £4 in cash.

D   C   and W   pleaded guilty to a further charge of entering 74a, Albany Road, on May 11, and stealing a radio cassette worth £34 and £14 in cash.

Det - Constable Graham Pickthorne, prosecuting, said that W   worked at Marlowe's Restaurant, Stratford, from December, 1976, to May, 1979, first as a waiter and then as restaurant manager.

Mr Roger Austen, defending M   and D   C   said that D   C   thought that W   was going to see a friend when he called at 74a, Albany

Road, on May 11 and didn't realise what was going on until they were inside the house.

Although she didn't take part in the burglary she did accept goods that had been stolen.

Both were short of money at the time of the second burglary, he said, and although they remained outside they agreed to try to sell the stolen radio-TV.

The magistrates adjourned sentence on the two girls until October 2, so that probation reports could be prepared.

Drink problem

Mr Michael Jervis, defending W   said that W   who was in breach of a probation order, had a drinking problem and had experimented with drugs.

But the theft from his employer had only come to light because he had confessed the theft to his probation officer.

W   was sentenced to a total of six months' imprisonment and disqualified from driving for 12 months. His licence was endorsed.

He was also fined £25 with an alternative of 14 days' imprisonment, for careless driving and £60, with an alternative of 14 days' imprisonment, for failing to provide a specimen. The magistrates ordered the prison sentences to run concurrently.

Clothes thief jailed

A COVENTRY man who admitted stealing and failing to surrender to bail was jailed for three months by Coventry magistrates yesterday.

E   W   (30), of Henley Green, Coventry, was charged with stealing £32-98 worth of clothing from

Owen Owen and £35-15 worth from Hoiles in Coventry.

W   also admitted failing to surrender to bail at the court on June 13.

The magistrates implemented three months of a suspended prison sentence to which W   was subject to run concurrently.

Police attacked by kiosk woman

POLICE who went to a telephone box at Wolston as the result of a 999 call at 2.15 a.m. were attacked by a woman.

At Rugby yesterday M   K   S   (44), of Bretford, admitted assaulting Policewoman Anna Marie Guthrie and Police Constable Robert Fell.

She also pleaded guilty to being in charge of a Land-Rover with excess alcohol in her blood, and to leaving a car with its headlights on.

Inspector Derrick Barrett

said that after pushing and biting the policewoman, S   went from the kiosk to the Land-Rover and got in the driver's seat. When P.C. Fell tried to remove the keys she kicked him.

An analysis showed 204mg. of alcohol in 100ml. of blood.

Mr John Kennedy, for S   said that she was ashamed of what had happened. She had been out to a pub with her husband, had had more drink at home and then when her husband had gone to bed "she had an overwhelming desire to speak to friends in Spain."

The kiosk near her home had been vandalised so she drove the Land-Rover to Wolston where she unaccountably dialled 999.

S   was fined £50 on each assault charge, £75 and banned for four months for being in charge of a vehicle with excess alcohol, and £10 for leaving the lights on. She was also ordered to pay £12.25 costs.

Unlicensed TV fines

SEVEN Coventry people were fined a joint total of £240 by the city magistrates for using television sets without licences.

Fined for using colour sets were: R   F   of Earlsdon (£46); Mrs M   E   of   Road (£16); Mrs D   W   of   Close (£43); E   L   of Pinley (£40); D   B   of Allesley Park (£34); Mrs S   T   of Allesley (£46).

W   J   of Stoke, was fined £15 for using an unlicensed black-and-white set.

Each defendant was ordered to pay £3 costs.

Sold stolen TVs worth £800

A COVENTRY mother who stole £800-worth of rented colour television sets was yesterday given suspended prison sentences and ordered to pay £300 restitution.

At an earlier hearing Mrs F   T   L   (37), of Radford, had admitted stealing a £200 set from D. F. Gibbs and a £150 set belong-

ing to Multi Broadcast. She asked for two similar offences to be considered.

The court was told that had sold the sets.

Yesterday she was given sentences totalling six months suspended for two years. The restitution figure comprised £75 to be paid to each of the four firms from whom a set had been stolen.

She was allowed to pay at the rate of £3 a week.

Dr Madeline Sharp, presiding, said that the magistrates were concerned that none of the sets had been recovered so that four companies were together £800 out of pocket.

Mr Kevin Coleman, defending, said that L   committed the offence because of financial difficulty.

occasions defendants have asked me as their lawyer whether there is any way they can prevent their name appearing in the paper and breathed sighs of relief when their case was transferred to one of the smaller courts where no reporter was present. Some defendants actually give as a reason for pleading guilty or not choosing jury trial the fear that they would run the risk of attracting more publicity if they did anything other than plead guilty in the magistrates' court. A Coventry *Evening Telegraph* reporter mentioned one defendant who even followed him back to his office after his case had been heard, offered the reporter a 'fiver' to keep his name out of the papers and, when this was refused, surreptitiously slipped the money into the reporter's pocket as he left the office.

Notes

1. A. E. Bottoms and J. D. McClean, *Defendants in the Criminal Process* (Routledge and Kegan Paul, London, 1976), p. 116.
2. M. Cain, *Society and the Policeman's Role* (Routledge and Kegan Paul, London, 1973).
3. Laurie, *Scotland Yard* (Bodley Head, London, 1970).
4. Laurie, ibid., p. 14.
5. Laurie, ibid.
6. M. Zander, 'Access to a Solicitor in the Police Station', *Criminal Law Review* (1972), p. 342.
7. J. Brown, *The Techniques of Persuasion* (Penguin, Harmondsworth, 1972).
8. Bottoms and McClean, *Defendants*, p. 115.
9. Cain, *Society and the Policeman's Role*, p. 117.
10. S. Dell, *Silent in Court* (Bell, London, 1971), p. 32.
11. Ibid., pp. 32-3.
12. Ibid., p. 33.
13. Bottoms and McClean, *Defendants*, p. 45.
14. Ibid., p. 46.
15. Ibid., p. 121.
16. Ibid., p. 121. See also C. Davies, 'The Innocent who Plead Guilty', *Law Guardian* (March 1970), p. 9.
17. Bottoms and McClean, *Defendants*, pp. 152-3.
18. Z. Bankowski and G. Mungham, *Images of Law* (Routledge and Kegan Paul, London, 1976), p. 63.
19. Bottoms and McClean, *Defendants*, pp. 154-60; H. Benson (Chairman), *Report of Royal Commission on Legal Services* (HMSO London, 1979), vol. 2, Part A, Section 8.
20. Bottoms and McClean, *Defendants*, pp. 156-60.
21. See evidence of Legal Action Group to Royal Commission on Legal Services, 1979.
22. M. King, *Duty Solicitors* (Cobden Trust, London, 1976), pp. 37-9.
23. Bankowski and Mungham, *Images of Law*, p. 52.
24. P. Carlen, *Magistrates' Justice* (Martin Robertson, London, 1976), p. 89.
25. See J. Baldwin and M. McConville, *Negotiated Justice* (Martin Robertson,

London, 1977).

26. See p. 65.

27. Criminal Justice Act 1948, Schedule 3.

28. The Streatfield Report, *Report of the Interdepartmental Committee on the Business of the Criminal Courts* (HMSO, London, 1961).

29. S. Perry, *Information for the Courts — a New Look at Social Inquiry Reports* (Cambridge Institute for Criminology, Cambridge, 1974), p. 64.

30. J. Thorpe, *Social Enquiry Reports* (HMSO, London 1979).

31. Ibid., pp. 15-16.

32. Ibid., p. 18.

33. Perry, *Information for the Courts*, p. 15.

34. Ibid., p. 18, Table 5.

35. Ibid., p. 95.

36. Ibid., p. 24.

37. See Carlen, *Magistrates' Justice*, p. 60 and Thorpe, *Social Enquiry Reports*, p. 16.

38. M. Davies, 'Social Enquiry Reports for the Courts', *British Journal of Criminology*, vol. 4, no. 1 (1974), pp. 18-31.

39. Perry, *Information for the Courts*, Ch. 3.

40. See P. Bean, *Rehabilitation and Deviance* (Routledge and Kegan Paul, London, 1976).

41. See W. White, 'The Presentation in Court of Social Inquiry Reports', *Criminal Law Review* (1971), p. 342.

42. J. Hine, W. McWilliams and K. Pease, 'Recommendations, Social Information and Sentencing', *Howard Journal*, vol. 17 (1978), pp. 91-100.

43. Thorpe, *Social Enquiry Reports*, p. 28 and Table B.

44. E. Burney, *J. P. — Magistrates' Court and Community* (Constable, London, 1979), pp. 116-19.

45. Carlen, *Magistrates' Justice*, p. 24.

46. See Home Office, *The Sentence of the Court* (HMSO, London, 1978). N. Walker, *Sentencing in a Rational Society* (Penguin, Harmondsworth, 1969).

47. D. Sudnow, 'Normal Crimes: Features of the Penal Code in a Public Defenders Office', *Social Problems*, vol. 12 (Winter 1965), pp. 255-75.

48. M. King, 'A Status Passage Analysis of the Defendant's Progress through the Magistrates' Court', *Law and Human Behaviour*, vol. 2, no. 3 (1978), p. 211.

49. Carlen, *Magistrates' Justice*, p. 126.

50. See J. Shapland, 'The Construction of a Mitigation' in D. Farrington, K. Hawkins and S. Lloyd-Bostock (eds.), *Psychology, Law and Legal Processes* (Macmillan, London, 1978).

51. S. White, 'Homilies in Sentencing', *Criminal Law Review* (1971), p. 90.

52. Burney, *J. P.*, p. 115.

53. Ibid.

54. Ibid., p. 113.

55. R. Bond and N. Lemon, 'Changes in Magistrates' Attitudes during the First Year on the Bench' in Farrington *et al.*, *Psychology, Law and Legal Processes*.

56. R. Tarling, *Sentencing Practices in Magistrates' Courts* (HMSO, London, 1979), p. 27.

57. Ibid., p. 29.

58. Burney, *J. P.*, p. 119 and see generally Ch. 9.

Making Sense of the System

1. Due Process

The principles of due process essential to any just system for the fair resolution of conflict if applied to a system for the prosecution and sentencing of offenders would manifest themselves in the rules of evidence, procedural rules and restrictions on the arbitrary use of power governing every aspect of the system from the treatment of suspects by police to the sentencing of defendants in court. According to due process ideals, not only should the rules exist, but they must be rigorously followed. Yet it is hard to think of any formal social situation in which the gap between rules and practice is wider than that between the Judges' Rules and the day-to-day practices of the police at police stations throughout the country. This does not mean that the present situation is necessarily unjust, for rules which were laid down some time ago may now fail to serve any useful purpose under modern social conditions and may indeed help to promote injustice for the victims of crime and ultimately for society. One has to go further and ask whether the actual police practices which contravene the Judges' Rules represent fair procedures for arriving at the truth or by contrast, the exercise of oppressive and arbitrary power. Clearly in some cases where the only contravention is, for example, in the denial of access to a solicitor before interrogation, it is arguable that no major infringement of basic rights has occurred, providing that the police questioning is fairly conducted, for the suspect, being fully aware of his rights, may decide to confess voluntarily. However, as we have seen, there is sufficient evidence to suggest that in practice the police in many cases go far beyond the simple isolation of the defendant for questioning, but include such tactics as deception, threats, inducements, solitary confinement, verbal and in some cases physical bullying.[1] In no circumstances could such conduct be considered compatible with principles of due process or with an ideological perspective which sees the police as agents for the resolution of social conflict. In the more blatant cases of abuse it could be argued that the police in their efforts to secure convictions create more injustice and social evil than those who are officially designated as criminals. Moreover the most that can be said for the Judges' Rules is that like unenforceable laws, they stand out as a symbol of society's concern for justice and fairness as admirable, but totally unrealised, ideals to which judges only pay lip-service while generally exercising their discretion to accept as evidence confessions made after the Rules had been contravened.

Due process sees a guilty plea as an honest admission that the defendant committed the offence. In most cases, it probably does represent just this, but, as recent research has shown, there are a disturbing number of defendants who having pleaded guilty, maintain that they did so not because they believed themselves to be guilty, but for reasons unrelated to their involvement in the offence.[2] These include a belief that the court will not believe them whatever they say, the knowledge that to contest the case will result in long delays and the expectation of a heavier than otherwise sentence should they be found guilty having pleaded not guilty.[3] In such cases the procedural safeguards and the most meticulous care of clerks and magistrates to ensure that the defendant understands the charge and the implications of his guilty plea will do nothing to prevent injustices from taking place.

In due process terms, moreover, the sentencing hearing determines the nature and extent of necessary legal intervention. The conflicts to be resolved are twofold. In the first place the demands of the victims of the crime for justice, that is retribution and compensation, must be balanced against the need to protect offenders against excessively severe punishments, which, while satisfying the victims, exceed the harm caused by the crime and the penalty he deserves while causing hardship to the defendant and his family. Secondly, the court must resolve the conflict between the individual's interests and those of the state. While the defendant seeks to minimise the effects of state intervention in his life, the state's concerns are to protect the community and to deter both the defendant and anyone who might be contemplating engaging in similar criminal activities.

If the ideals implicit in this approach are to be achieved, there must be a fair and thorough investigation by the court of the facts of the case in order to establish the degree of harm caused by the defendant's acts, the extent to which he is a dangerous person whom the state must restrain for the benefit of the community and the level of his personal responsibility for the crime. The three concepts of harm, dangerousness and responsibility which form the theoretical basis for distinguishing between the various levels of criminal behaviour, are indeed present in the gradations of statutory penalties for different offences but apart from some motoring cases where compulsory disqualification applies, the magistrates as we have seen have an enormous discretion over the severity and type of sentence imposed. The only limits to that discretion are the statutory maxima which for example prevent magistrates from imposing a borstal sentence or a prison term of longer than six months.[4]

In order that the court's decision-making process be fair and thorough, it is important that no evidence should be introduced into the courtroom which cannot be proved according to the strict rules of evidence, for these rules have been specifically formulated to exclude anything which could be unreliable or open to fabrication.[5] In addition, procedural due process dictates that both sides, prosecution and defence, should be given every opportunity to present their evidence and arguments and to challenge the case for the opposition. The decision which eventually emerges from this painstaking process should, according to this perspective, ideally be based on unequivocal facts and not on opinion, hearsay or value judgements.

It is clear from the evidence presented earlier that sentencing hearings in magistrates' courts fall short in several respects of the ideals of due process implicit in the court's role as promoter of justice and resolver of conflicts. For a start, many defendants face the court without the assistance of a legal representative, which immediately places them at a disadvantage and creates an imbalance between prosecution and defence. In most cases the decision as to whether a particular defendant should be represented is left to the magistrates and their clerk, so that the very people who are responsible for choosing the sentence also have a hand in determining the nature of the enquiry leading to the sentencing decision — a situation which in itself appears to conflict with the basic principle of equality between the parties, for the magistrates and their clerk have no part in deciding whether the police should have a lawyer to represent them.

Secondly, the formal rules of evidence are generally waived for sentencing hearings with the result that 'facts' on which the magistrates are required to decide sentence may be mere hearsay or opinion. Moreover, such evidence often goes unchallenged either because the defendant is unrepresented (and having had little or no experience of courtrooms and no warning of what the policeman or probation officer is going to say in court, is ill-equipped and ill-prepared to correct these official versions of the 'facts') or because the defence lawyer considers it to be tactically advisable not to accuse the policeman of lying or the probation officer of presenting to the court a distorted portrait of the defendant.[6]

Thirdly, as we have seen in the earlier discussion of guilty pleas, even such seemingly straightforward matters as the charges against the defendant may be the result of behind-the-scenes negotiations rather than reflecting with any accuracy the seriousness of his illegal conduct, his responsibility for the crime or his dangerousness to the community. The same 'low-visibility' processes may result in the editing of the evidence and distorting of 'facts' on which the magistrates ultimately base their sentencing decision. The police, as we have seen, may decide to 'put in a good word' for the defendant by stating for example that he co-operated with them or showed remorse. Furthermore, those defendants who are adequately represented by a solicitor or barrister, as well as having the advantage of a pre-trial strategist and negotiator may also benefit from a plea in mitigation which minimises their responsibility for the crime and seeks to find reasons in their social and psychological background for regarding them as unfortunates rather than evil-doers.[7]

The same may be true of the probation officer's contribution. The way in which some defendants are singled out for social enquiry reports owes little to principles of fairness and justice, but is rather an arbitrary process based on the subjective evaluation of individual magistrates. Whether or not the probation officer's report is favourable may also be the product of chance, deception and subjective evaluations, for much seems to depend upon how the defendant presents himself at the interview. There is little doubt that some of those defendants who end up being offered probation by the court are no less deserving of punishment than those who were not selected for social enquiry reports or those who, having been selected, failed to impress the probation officer.

It is perhaps easy to exaggerate the gap between ideals and practice in the sentencing process. No doubt there are cases where all the principles of due process are respected and the magistrates reach decisions which fairly balance the competing interests of victim, individual and state. What is clear, however, is that a model based on the justice function of the court, while it may help to guide magistrates in their sentencing decisions, tells us very little about the dynamics of the courtroom process. It tells us even less about the way in which the police handle suspects or about the interplay of the court professionals which often determines the manner in which the case is presented to the magistrates. The most that can be said is that the principles of due process are present in the rules, but even these rules give the police and magistrates adequate scope for exercising their discretion in ways which depart fundamentally from a strict justice approach.

2. Crime Control

While due process principles may be embodied within the administrative directions governing police questioning, the restrictions on powers of imprisonment and custodial remands and the procedural rules for courtroom hearings, by no means all formal rules are inspired by due process values. Some are rather the result of the desire to provide the police and magistrates with weapons with which to fight crime. Indeed, some formal rules expressly abrogate or suspend the rights of individual citizens by giving the police and the courts explicit powers, such as those of search, arrest, fingerprinting, detention for interrogation, custodial remands and the attaching of conditions to bail.

Frequently, however, crime control powers are not made explicit by the rules. Rather the police and courts are able to exercise them because the rules are left deliberately vague or do not cover specifically the situation in question. This allows the police and those magistrates who see their role primarily as that of controlling crime the opportunity to fill the gaps through the subjective exercise of their discretion. Examples of vague rules are the police power to hold suspects without charging them, to deny bail from the police station where the case is *a serious one*, the law excluding confessions which were made as the result of *oppression* and the police power to refuse a suspect access to a solicitor where this would cause *unreasonable delay or hindrance* to the process of investigation or the administration of justice.

Tacit powers are also possible where the rules themselves carry no legislative weight and where no sanction is imposed on their contravention. Examples of 'weightless' rules at the pre-trial stage are of course the Judges' Rules which, as we have seen, are mere administrative directions. Moreover, there are also vague and 'weightless' rules at the sentencing stage. These purport to restrict the powers of the magistrates, but in reality are merely symbolic reminders of policy ideals. They include the restriction on sending offenders under 21 to prison unless all alternative punishments have been considered and rejected by the magistrates and the limit and the passing of a suspended sentence and community service orders to cases where the magistrates would normally have imposed a prison sentence. Furthermore, sentencing in magistrates' courts is essentially a discretionary process which gives ample scope to the magistrates to impose deterrent and examplary punishment to further the interests of crime control.

It is crime control values which lie behind most of the infringements of a suspect's rights and dignity which regularly occur at police stations. Although the objective of most of these infringements is to obtain confessions and hence convictions which are essential to the effectiveness of the crime control function of the criminal justice system, this is not always the case. It is clear that some behaviour that takes place has little to do with obtaining confessions or evidence for use in court, but are rather deliberate attempts to deter the suspect from future criminal activities through a combination of humiliation and intimidation by verbal and physical abuse.

It is possible also to interpret several aspects of the courtroom sentencing hearing as direct deterrents designed to shock and humiliate the defendant and so discourage him from further involvement in crime. These include such obvious unpleasant treatment as his isolation in court as an object of attention and ridicule and the exposure of his shameful behaviour, but they may also involve less clear instances of 'punishment' as in the public revelation of private information about the defendant, such as his age, his disabilities, his level of intelligence, his family and employment situations and his financial position. Adding to the unpleasantness of the hearing the magistrates' homily often takes the form of a stern reprimand and warning of what will happen to the defendant if he continues to engage in a life of crime. The fact that these homilies are reminiscent of a stern parent's attempt to make his or her child behave tends to reduce the defendant to a childlike figure which may further serve to humiliate him and so, in theory, at least, deter him.

According to this perspective anyone whose role conflicts with that of controlling crime is regarded essentially as obstructing the achievement of the real purpose of the courtroom process. Defence lawyers, therefore, are unnecessary luxuries whose only useful functions are to provide the proceedings with a due process gloss. As such, they are thoroughly expendable and should be employed only where absolutely necessary to retain public confidence in the criminal courts. Moreover, much of the information which both defence lawyers and probation officers present to the court is irrelevant to the court's deterrent function. Indeed, the only important evidence for punishment purposes is that which indicates the degree of the defendant's participation in the crime, his previous record and the most effective punishment for special and general deterrence. Likewise strict rules of evidence and procedure may stand in the way of the court's deterrent function by prolonging proceedings, complicating 'simple' issues and excluding important information such as details known to the police about the defendant's previous criminal activities which, for one reason or another, did not result in convictions.

Probation officers may in some cases be effective agents for crime control to the extent that they are able to exercise a degree of supervision over the lives of offenders and to prevent them re-engaging in criminal activities. In general, however, those who advocate a crime control function for the courts are sceptical about the effectiveness of probation and other rehabilitation measures. Furthermore the roles played by defence lawyers and probation officers and the impediments resulting from the rules of evidence and procedure may have an even more serious impact than merely inconveniencing and frustrating the police and prosecution. Frequently the magistrates will be reluctant to impose a sentence which is sufficiently severe to have any real deterrent value either because they have been persuaded by an eloquent plea in mitigation or a sympathetic social enquiry report that harsh punishment is not appropriate or because the prosecution have been prevented by the rules from presenting the dependant's 'true character' to the court. Since the certainty of severe punishment if caught and convicted is an essential feature of the deterrence paradigm, any forbearance by the magistrates in this regard may be seen as weakening the efficiency of the court as an agency for crime control.

Thus, to the extent that the court does substitute other objectives to that of punishment pure and simple, the crime control model fails to account for every aspect of the sentencing process. Yet in general it does provide a remarkably accurate model of the actual operation of the criminal justice process as it relates to defendants who plead guilty at the magistrates' courts. For most of them, particularly the first and second time defendants, the proceedings are indeed unpleasant and humiliating. Only a minority have lawyers or probation officers present to act as their protectors and agents in their dealings with the court, and the protection they offer is often illusory. The remainder, as we have seen, are sentenced to punishments for the most part on the basis of the information provided by the police. Whether or not they are represented, the punishments inflicted by the court tend to reflect the tariff which takes into account the seriousness of the offence and the defendant's previous convictions. Apart from the formal punishment of the court's sentence and the 'unofficial' punishments arising from the defendant's treatment at the hands of the police and in the courtroom there are often deterrents associated with criminal justice, which although not defined as punishments by either the defendant or the regular court participants nevertheless may be as subjectively as unpleasant to many defendants as the courtroom degradation or the formal sentence. These include the loss of earnings involved in attending court, the delays and uncertainty which epitomise the criminal justice process, and the shame and embarrassment of having to reveal to one's family, employer or friends that one is involved in criminal proceedings. Even after the case is over, some defendants will be affected by repercussions from the proceedings which are not strictly punishments, such as losing one's job, having to pay out contributions towards the prosecution's legal costs or the legal aid costs of one's own lawyer. Finally, there is the disgrace of having one's name and misdeeds published in the local newspaper.

3. Bureaucratic

This perspective, it will be recalled, views the criminal justice process as essentially neutral in the conflict between prosecution and defence and between the state and the individual. It is concerned rather with the efficient management of the demands created by crime, criminals and the social agencies charged with handling them. Bureaucratic values emphasise the saving of time and expense and the encouragement of order, uniformity and predictability within the system.

Perhaps the clearest examples of bureaucratic principles in operation arising from the evidence set out in Chapters 3 and 4 relate to the need for practicality and economy in a system where resources are severely restricted. For the police, therefore, the cheapest, quickest way of obtaining convictions is by persuading suspects to confess and defendants to plead guilty. Thus a considerable amount of police effort goes into interrogation and the securing of signed statements from suspects.[8] Similarly, it is practical and economical for solicitors to confine their work activities to set office hours and to a fixed location. It is perhaps not surprising, therefore, that few of them are prepared to attend police stations at night, or that they may try to cram as many cases as possible into a morning at the magistrates' court.[9] Probation officers too may be constrained by heavy case-loads to the extent that they may be tempted to take short-cuts in the preparation of social enquiry reports, relying on second-hand information or providing the court with little more than superficial impressions.[10]

In their relationships with one another the courtroom regulars are constantly reflecting bureaucratic values. The view held by many of them that the exchanges between them should not merely be restrained and cordial, but warm and friendly, and the agreements and favours that arise from these exchanges are indicative of the effectiveness of the court social network in managing tension and keeping conflict to a minimum. The network also provides negative reinforcement by ridiculing and ostracising those who 'make trouble' or 'take things too seriously'.[11] The maintenance of friendly relationships is important for the pursuit of bureaucratic ideals, not simply for its tension-management function. In addition, it assists in promoting courtroom efficiency, since it enables the participants to know in advance through their informal interchanges what is likely to be said about the defendant in court.

For the court to work effectively as a bureaucratic machinery, one would expect to find sophisticated techniques for socialising outsiders who approach the court unaware of its rules and conventions. Such outsiders may, of course, include novice regulars or those who have not previously appeared at that particular court, but the group which presents the greatest threat to courtroom efficiency is clearly the defendants, for as well as being generally unfamiliar with the formalities and artificialities of the courtroom procedure, they are often in a state of heightened anxiety or antagonism towards the police. One such technique is to provide the outsider with a 'tutor', someone who is able to ensure that the outsider obeys the rules of the organisation, while at the same time maintaining that his tutoring is for the benefit of the outsider. In the magistrates' court, it is usually the defence lawyer who takes on this role, although on occasions the task might fall to a probation or police officer. In magistrates' courts defence lawyers have the additional advantage of minimising the defendant's own contribution to the courtroom hearing and so his potential for disruption by speaking 'on his behalf'. However, the provision of a defence lawyer for every defendant would be extremely costly. Furthermore, some such lawyers are a mixed blessing, for they may on occasions raise the level of tension in the courtroom or prolong the hearing unnecessarily, both of which run contrary to the achievement of bureaucratic ideals. One might reasonably expect to find, therefore, other methods, cheaper, but equally effective, by which the organisation controls outsiders.

Clearly, many of the features of the courtroom process described in Chapter 4 may be interpreted in this way. There is the sapping of the defendant's competence through his isolation in the dock and subjection to unfamiliar rules of discourse. There are the reinforcements in the form of instructions and interruptions from the clerk or magistrate, should defendants fail to plead or answer questions adequately or if they attempt to introduce 'irrelevancies', such as accusations against the police. There are also the organisational discouragements against pleading not guilty, the long delays and the possibility of extra costs and a heavier sentence which are risked when a defendant decides to contest the case against him. Since the court has the power to impose sanctions on the defendant, it may use this power to increase organisational efficiency either by threatening a disruptive defendant or by rewarding the compliant, co-operative defendant. Another technique for avoiding problems that might be caused by outsiders is as far as possible to ignore the outsider altogether. This is certainly possible where the defendant is legally represented. Even where he has no lawyer, the magistrates or clerk may, as we have seen, prefer information about him to come in the form of official records from the police, probation office or court files rather than from the defendant's own mouth.[12]

Applying the bureaucratic model, therefore, the courtroom performance of the clerk, or in stipendiary courts, the magistrate, may be interpreted as having a socialisation function, the objective of the socialisation being to ensure that the hearing progresses with maximum efficiency to a conclusion which cannot be faulted by reference to the formal rules. These rules themselves may also have the effect of promoting efficiency and managing tension within the courtroom. In the case of the rules of procedure, there is clearly the intention to produce orderly proceedings, providing the prosecution the opportunity to place before the court all the facts in its possession concerning the circumstances of the offence and the character of the offender and affording to the defence the chance to challenge and correct information from the prosecution and to present arguments and evidence favourable to the defendant so as to mitigate the sentence. In fact these rules do more than produce orderly proceedings. Through their insistence on highly formalised turn-taking they help to ensure that open conflict is kept to the minimum. Defendants, for example, who disagree strongly with the facts presented by the police are effectively forbidden from challenging them in face-to-face confrontation, except through the highly ritualised asking of questions. Only after the prosecution has closed its case and the offending policeman has resumed his seat at the rear of the courtroom may the defendant put his version to the court.

The ease with which much that happens both inside and outside the courtroom in uncontested cases may be neatly slotted into a bureau-cratic interpretation may give the impression that this model of the criminal justice process is able to account for almost anything related to magistrates' courts, except perhaps where formal contests take place over, for example, bail or guilt. This, however, ignores the fact that there are several important features of the criminal justice pro-cess in these courts which on the face of things appear detrimental to efficiency and the promotion of bureaucratic objectives. These in-clude the very presence of the defendant in the courtroom. If the only purpose was to process cases as speedily as possible with the minimum of disruption, it would surely be much more convenient to the pro-fessionals involved to proceed on the basis of information provided orally and in writing from the courtroom regulars, as happens in appellate courts and Parole Board hearings. If the sentencing decision could be made just as efficiently in the defendant's absence, as it is in uncontested motoring cases, then his presence in court is only ex-plicable in terms other than those provided by the bureaucratic model. Other features which seem inconsistent with the fulfilment of bureau-cratic objectives include the time and effort spent in many cases on ensuring that the defendant has understood the charges and has plead-ed correctly, in listening patiently to character witnesses or the defen-dant himself, when the information they give is unlikely to influence the final decision and, above all, in determining the 'appropriate' sentence. Such application of manpower and resources may seem particularly surprising, given the fact that there is no evidence to suggest that a more mechanical, less time-consuming process would achieve less effective results, at least in terms of reconviction rates. Furthermore the trend in recent years has been in the direction of broadening the sentencing discretion by increasing the alternatives available to the magistrates, which, seen from a purely instrumental viewpoint, would appear to detract from organisational efficiency.

It is clear that bureaucratic considerations, although an important factor in the operation of magistrates' courts in their handling of guilty pleaders, represent part only of the philosophical make-up of the courtroom professionals and decision-makers. Perhaps it is fair to say that considerations of efficiency and cost-benefit effectiveness, while never far from the consciousness of clerks, lawyers, policemen, probation officers and magistrates, usually take second place to more pressing demands arising from the particular ideologies each of these groups subscribe to in the course of their role performances within the criminal justice system, be they due process, crime control, rehabilitation or otherwise. Yet, when these ideological demands are weak or are ignored or neglected by these actors, it is usually the organisational considerations for effective processing of cases which come to the fore.

4. Medical

It is clearly beyond the resources of the state to apply the medical model to each of the thousands of defendants who appear before the criminal courts, for this would involve a huge number of highly qualified diagnosing and rehabilitation experts and the provision of many hundreds of treatment programmes. A modified medical model has therefore evolved. This model makes it permissible for the court to select for treatment only those defendants who are likely to benefit from rehabilitation measures.[13]

This modified approach also allows the court to interpret any reconviction following a treatment programme as a failure on the part of the defendant to respond to the treatment or to seize the opportunity that was offered him, rather than a failure by those responsible for carrying out the treatment or the general ineffectiveness of the treatment programme in dealing with his problems. In this somewhat strange manner, therefore, the court may succeed in retaining the notion that the defendant is personally responsible for his conduct while nevertheless accepting the idea that treatment rather than punishment is the answer to his particular problem.[14] Thus, although punishment should play no part in the pursuit of the rehabilitative ideal were the medical model strictly applied, it is clear that according to the modified model the court may set narrow limits on the use of rehabilitation, first, by invoking it only in selected cases and, secondly, by reverting to deterrence and the control of crime through punishment whenever the treatment proves ineffective or the defendant declines to co-operate with the treatment regime.

Even in the 'worthy' cases where the eventual sentence may have a rehabilitative goal, any attempt to interpret the criminal justice process prior to sentence purely in terms of the rehabilitative ideals of expert analysis, diagnosis and prognosis is beset by problems. In the first place, what happens to a defendant before the sentencing hearing may be in direct contradiction to the goal of the rehabilitation. In some cases, for example, detention in the police cells or remands in custody, as well as being unpleasant for the defendant, may conflict directly with the treatment which the court may eventually decide to be appropriate. In other words, while the knowledge of the negative effect of a custodial sentence, such as loss of employment, accommodation and the disintegration of the defendant's family may be a strong factor in influencing the magistrates to impose a sentence which is more conducive to rehabilitation, the defendant may already have experienced before sentencing the same negative effects which the court now scrupulously seeks to avoid. A more general contradiction lies in the treatment that most suspects can expect to receive at the hands of the police. In very few cases can one seriously describe such treatment as meeting the suspect's needs or helping him with his problems. Secondly, the information which the police provide to the court in the form of antecedents and 'brief facts' is also likely to do little to further the cause of rehabilitation. Indeed, on occasions it may even obstruct the magistrates in achieving this objective in giving a distorted account of the defendant's background and his criminal activities. Sometimes, as we have seen, the police withdraw or reduce charges in return for guilty pleas.[15] More frequently they offer the court an account of the defendant's motivation either directly in their 'brief facts' or through suggestions which find their way into confessions made by the defendant under police guidance. Both may help to present to the magistrates a highly subjective impression of the defendant. Nor is the information provided by defence lawyers any more likely to contribute to the diagnostic process, for the role of the lawyer, in sentencing hearings, is to mitigate, and their pleas in mitigation reflect their wish to mimimise the impact of the intervention of the criminal justice process in the defendant's life rather than provide the court with the sort of objective, reliable information that would assist it to provide for the defendant's needs which may possibly involve a high level of intervention. Moreover, where the defendant is unrepresented, it is even less likely that the magistrates will be presented with useful information for the court's rehabilitative role. The threatening atmosphere of the courtroom, his isolation from other participants to the hearing and the curt questions from magistrates and their clerks are unlikely to inspire the majority of defendants to overcome their nervousness and shed their inhibitions so as to disclose freely and candidly facts about themselves which might lead to an accurate assessment and the eventual solution of their 'problems'.

In many cases, therefore, the criminal justice process from arrest to sentence by the magistrates may proceed without any attempt whatsoever to apply the principles derived from the medical model. However, it should follow that where the court decides that a probation officer, the court 'rehabilitation expert', should prepare a report on the defendant, this, at least, is some indication that the court is attempting to find a sentence that will meet the defendant's needs. Yet, when one examines closely the actual content of social enquiry reports and the influence of these reports on sentencing it becomes clear that what is going on bears very little resemblance to the objective diagnosis of illness and search for an effective treatment. The information contained in the social enquiry report, as we have seen, is often extremely sketchy and in many cases only the minimal steps have been taken to verify this information.[16] Furthermore, the probation officer's recommendation may be based in part upon his subjective response to the defendant and in part on what he considers the court would accept as a reasonable sentence in all the circumstances. On occasions the social enquiry report may even come very close to resembling a plea in mitigation with the probation officer actually suppressing information which is likely to be unfavourable to the defendant.[17]

Nevertheless, all the studies that have been conducted in this area suggest that the social enquiry reports, particularly those containing a specific recommendation, do carry considerable weight at the sentencing hearing.[18] The information contained in the report is usually regarded as an objective account of the defendant's background prepared by an impartial expert. Moreover, this information is rarely tested through the sort of extensive cross-examination that is applied to all other forms of evidence. Furthermore, although the defence solicitor may express his disagreement with the probation officer's recommendation, he will not in any way attempt to undermine the probation officer's status as an expert.

To summarise, therefore, the objective of rehabilitation and the principles derived from the medical model conflict with the traditional role of the criminal justice system. Even in those 'worthy' cases where the defendant is in need of help and treatment, there remain many features which are more in keeping with the objectives of punishment and crime control than with those of rehabilitation. These include police practices as interrogators and investigators, the formal, intimidating atmosphere of the courtroom and the fact that sentences are decided by people who are supposed to represent community values rather than by trained experts in penology. It is as if the court's welfare role had been imposed upon the traditional structure without any fundamental changes being made to that structure. Historically, this is more or less what happened when probation officers became compilers of social information about the offender and sentencing advisers.

5. Status Passage

The status passage model goes beyond the more obvious interpretations of the criminal justice process and attempts to relate the situations created inside and outside the courtrooms to a general theory concerning the hierarchy of individuals within society. According to this model, therefore, the objective of the court is not merely the neutral processing of criminals in as smooth and efficient manner as possible; nor is it simply punishing people for deterrent and retributive reasons. The status passage perspective rather sees the central aims of the criminal justice process as the imposition of a new social status on all or almost all defendants. In seeking to achieve this objective, all those involved in criminal justice are engaged in the task of reducing the defendant to a symbol within a recurrent social ritual. This is not the same as making life unpleasant for defendants, although the efforts to lower his status may well have the additional effect of shaming and humiliating him.[19] What are the features of the criminal justice process relating to defendant's pleading guilty in magistrates' courts which fit this interpretation of events?

To begin with, much of what happens to suspects at the police station may be interpreted as an exercise in degradation. Loss of control of the timing of the fulfilment of the most basic of human needs, food, drink, sleep, urinating, facing accusations and criticisms of conduct, often accompanied by insults and threats of punishment, and, finally subjection to searching, fingerprints and photographing— all have the effect of robbing a person of his self-confidence, his self-esteem and his individuality. Furthermore the knowledge among the suspect's family, friends, work-mates or employers that he has been arrested or is 'helping the police with their enquiries' may, whether or not he is actually charged with and convicted of a criminal offence, serve to lower his social standing in the eyes of the community. Alternatively, the defendant's private degradation behind the closed doors of the police station may be seen as a preliminary to the public denunciation ceremony, a dress rehearsal for the courtroom performance when the defendant is prepared for or socialised into the passive role he will be expected to play throughout the remainder of his involvement in the criminal justice system.

According to the status passage model, the courtroom regulars, while appearing to play out very different roles, are in fact engaged together in the pursuit of the overriding objectives of the denunciation and degradation of the defendant. In the case of defendants who plead guilty, there is ample evidence to support this view. In the first place, we have already remarked on the way in which most solicitors are quite content to allow the police to have their way at the police station, offering little or no attempt to interfere with police persuasive tactics which might well determine the outcome of the case in court.

Secondly we have seen how the defendant, once he appears in court to be sentenced, is placed outside the legitimate moral order by the policeman or prosecuting solicitor who presents the court with the 'brief facts of the case', for as well as setting out the defendant's illicit behaviour, these 'facts' will often include a confession or informal admission of guilt which, more often than not, indicates the 'cause' of that behaviour, be it drunkenness, shortage of money, boredom, revenge, etc. We have indicated how the police usually 'help' suspects with the wording of these confessions and with the 'explanations' presented in court for their behaviour. As these confessions are usually framed in such a way as to 'go down well with the bench', they reflect inevitably the court's prevailing view of criminal causality. Whatever the prevailing view may be, if the defendant wishes to win the sympathy of the bench, he must in the explanation he gives to the police or direct to the magistrates in court accept the legitimacy of the existing legal order and place himself outside that order. This involves an acknowledgement that his behaviour was wrong and that he deserved to be punished for it. As in the case of Mr Grant,[20] attempts to escape from the role of the denounced and to re-establish one's position as a person who is no different from other people are vehemently resisted.

A third example is the role of the defence lawyer in court. Although he is officially the mouthpiece of his client, his success in mitigating the court's sentence depends to a significant degree upon his willingness to contribute to the denunciation of the defendant. This paradoxical nature of the lawyer's role means that trying 'too hard' for his client may well have the reverse of the intended effect. Once the defendant has pleaded guilty, the defence lawyer must publically accept the legitimacy of the courtroom hearing and refrain from any attempt to challenge the law of the legal process.[21] Yet while they may challenge some of the minor details of the prosecution case, most defence lawyers, as we have seen, will interpret their responsibility for representing their client's interests by apologising on the defendant's behalf and offering an explanation which portrays their client as pathological, that is essentially different and qualitively inferior to 'normal' law-abiding citizens.[22] Thus, at the same time as he promotes his client's interests, the lawyer adds his contribution to the denunciation ceremony and helps to ensure its success.[23]

Fourthly, the probation officer may be seen as playing a very similar role to that of the defence lawyer, although his motivation and philosophical approach to the sentencing hearing may be very different. Whatever the recommendation the probation officer may have in his social enquiry report and whatever his portrayal of the defendant on which the recommendation was made, it is almost inevitable that by the time sentence is passed, he will have contributed to the success of the courtroom degradation. Put in its most basic terms, there is the implication every time that the court asks for a social enquiry report that the defendant is bad, mad or in need of help. Of the three categories the third is obviously the least damaging to a person's status, but even here stigma attaches to the person who is defined as socially so incompetent that it is necessary for the court to appoint an official specifically to supervise his or her behaviour. The only way that the probation officer is to escape from the task of denouncing the defendant is by blaming factors outside the defendant's control for his criminal conduct. Although this device may succeed on rare occasions, if the probation officer uses it too often, he runs the serious risk of losing credibility with the court and having his sentencing recommendation ignored, since his view of causality, responsibility and pathology will be quite out of line with that of the magistrates and other courtroom regulars. In other words, the 'closed loop' described on page 79, which is essential for a good working relationship between the courts and the probation service, will be conspicuously absent.

Quite apart from the performance of the actors, the status passage model would lead one to expect to find features of the courtroom ceremony, the centrepiece of the degradation process which has the intrinsic function of portraying the defendant as a 'person apart', reflecting his new status as a degraded individual. In the magistrates' court there is, in the first place, the defendant's physical isolation from everyone else in the courtroom through the use and strategic placing of the dock. Even those defendants who, because of the minor nature of their offence, are not actually placed in the dock, must nevertheless stand directly in front of it, rather than sitting next to their lawyers. Secondly, there are the special ways of addressing the offender and referring to him, peculiar to his courtroom identity as a person who is about to be or who has been denounced.[24] Finally, the general effect of the formal law and rules of procedure, as we have seen, is to inhibit and often restrict altogether the defendant's active participation in the hearing. The less he speaks out for himself, the greater his dependence upon the courtroom professionals who will almost inevitably attempt to define him and his conduct in terms which will accentuate the difference between him and 'law-abiding citizens' and thus enhance the degradation ceremony. According to Garfinkel, the success of the degradation ceremony depends not only on the treatment of the person to be denounced, but also upon the perceived status of the denouncer. He must be regarded as 'a publicly know person';

> He must not portray himself as acting according to his personal, unique experiences. He must rather be regarded as acting in his capacity as a public figure, drawing upon communally entertained and verified experience . . .
>
> The denouncer must make the dignity of the supra-personal values of the tribe salient and accessible to view, and his denunciation must be delivered in their name.[25]

The lay magistrate, being both 'an ordinary member of the community' and an official appointed by the Crown, combines the two attributes which Garfinkel believes to be essential for a successful denouncer. Although lay justices say very little during sentencing by comparison with stipendiaries and Crown Court judges, when they do speak, it is often either to emphasise the personal responsibility of the defendant for his actions or to give credence to the ideal that they are applying community values acting for the good of the community in their decision-making. Both reinforce the denunciation objectives of the ceremony. In the case of stipendiary magistrates the belief must be rather in their inherent authority as appointed officials and the capacity as wise, just men to give expression to the values of the community in their decisions.[26]

In order to have any impact the degradation ceremony must affect the defendant's self-esteem and the attitude of others towards him outside the immediate confines of the court. A guilty person, according to the status passage model is not permitted to resume his place in the community as if the courtroom ceremony had never taken place. There need to be, therefore, effective methods of communicating the fact of the defendant's degradation and denunciation to the out-

side world. In English magistrates' courts the two official communication media are, as we have seen, the press and the police. By selecting
those cases which are likely to be of interest to their readers, the press
may be seen as enhancing the status passage objectives of the court, for
those defendants who attract the stigma of the community either
through their heinous offences or through their high social status are
the ones most likely to have their cases reported. The police role in
informing employers, although rather less haphazard and more dis-
criminating than the press, may nevertheless be interpreted in the
same manner. They transmit details of the denunciation to the community in those cases where they perceive that there is a danger to the
public arising from the defendant's activities. Just as the police may
exercise their function of arbiters of public morality, in their decision
on whether or not to prosecute in a particular case, so do they in their
choice of cases for information to be passed to employers. The way
in which they exercise this discretion is outside the scope of this enquiry, but suffice it to remark that the police view of dangerousness
and public concern is not always one supported by every sector of the
community. Ultimately, however, the decision whether to take any
action on the defendant's conviction by dismissing him or demoting
him will be left to the employer and his or her judgement of the defendant's dangerousness.

Although the notion that they are engaged in an exercise of denunciation and degradation does not spring readily to the minds of the
actors involved in the magistrates' court process, some would argue
that the features we have identified as conforming to a status passage
interpretation of the courtroom sentencing hearing are no more than
by-products of the other, more obvious functions of magistrates'
courts. However, when one compares these courts with say the lower
criminal courts in the United States, it becomes apparent, first, that
the dock, the separation of the defendant from his lawyer and everyone else in the courtroom, is peculiar to the English courts. Secondly,
in American courts also little emphasis is placed upon the formal plea
in mitigation, since sentences in minor cases are often agreed before
the hearing between the District Attorney and defence counsel,
and the judge will frequently set his seal of approval to such agreements.[27] Where the defence counsel does mitigate, his client may make
his own contribution even to the extent of interrupting his lawyer to
correct facts or impressions given to the courts, unlike the English
court where the defendant must remain throughout a silent onlooker.
Thirdly, there are no special places for the press in most of the lower

criminal courts in the United States. Most cases which start and end in these courts are not reported in the local newspapers. The reason for these differences may be partly historical in that the layout and procedures in English magistrates' courts date back to a time when defendants usually appeared in police custody and few, if any, had lawyers to represent them. History alone does not, however, explain why these physical features have been retained in magistrates' courts built in the last ten years or why no attempt has been made to change court procedures so that they are less humiliating for the defendant. Nor do the usual justifications of the creation and maintenance of dignity and respect for the court provide a sufficient explanation for the retention of these features.

6. Power

The first point that is worth making is that, perhaps more than the other models, there are certain features of the system which, while readily interpretable in terms of the power model, are equally susceptible to other interpretations. One obvious feature is the social background of the magistrates.[28] Clearly, the fact that the majority of them come from the middle classes and the contrast between their background and that of most defendants supports the view of the system implicit in the power model. However, it is just as readily amenable to the interpretation that the decisions required of magistrates today are so complex that it is necessary to select people who have achieved a high educational level and positions in society where they are accustomed to exercising responsibility. This obviously creates a bias in favour of the middle classes. Similarly, alternative interpretations to those offered may be placed on many of the features discussed in this section, but this in itself does not invalidate the power model or the conception of reality which invokes.

Central to this approach is the notion that much of what passes for fairness, equality and humanity within the criminal justice system is nothing less than a sham to conceal its true coercive nature. One would look, therefore, for gaps between the rhetoric of the system, the face it presents to the world and the realities of its day-to-day operation. One would look also for efforts to conceal these unsalubrious aspects of the system from the public gaze. A clear example of this gulf between rhetoric and reality is to be found in the contrast between the formal courtroom hearing and the treatment of defendants at police stations.

On the one hand, there are all the formal trappings of legality, the rules of procedure, the presence of legal representatives, the strict restrictions on the use of power, the ritual of the public performance. On the other, there is the stark imposition of the coercive power of the state, in secret, without formal rules to protect suspects and without legal representation. The 'weightlessness' of the Judges' Rules, the police discretion not to admit or contact solicitors and the very existence of 'delayed confessors' all add force to the descriptions by defendants of the physical and psychological pressures which, they allege, the police impose.

Another example is the gap between the situation that an analysis of the formal rules would reveal and the day-to-day realities of the process. We have seen how the rules afford the defendant every opportunity to require the prosecution to prove its case against him beyond reasonable doubt; should he voluntarily forego this opportunity and plead guilty, the rules permit him to place before the court any matters which might be relevant to the sentencing decision. Even in the most simple case the defendant is faced with these two major decisions: how to plead and what to say in mitigation. In addition, a large number of important strategic points arise during the course of the guilty-pleader's progress through the magistrates' court ranging from deciding whether or not to apply for legal aid to considering whether to challenge the police 'brief facts'. Each of the points demands from the defendant a knowledge and experience, which the formal system assumes to exist, but which few defendants in practice possess. Rarely, therefore, is the defendant a competent decision-maker and tactician in his own case. Certainly, the rules treat him as an equal in every way to the prosecution, but, as Isaac Balbus says, 'to treat unequals equally is scarcely just'.[29] Certainly, most of them understand the literal meaning of the choices before them, but, to quote a police inspector in Pat Carlen's study, 'of course, they might not understand the advantages of one or the other'.[30] Quite apart from their ability to understand the full implications of their decisions, the assumption implicit in the formal rules that each defendant is a free agent to decide according to his conscience and to accept full responsibility for his decisions is also undermined by the realities of the situation. We have seen how, for example, guilty pleas may reflect not simply the defendant's historical guilt, but also the efforts of others to persuade him to plead guilty and the sanctions in the form of delays and additional costs and punishments lying in wait for those who contest the case against them.[31]

Of course, it is always open to the defendant to hire himself a strategic expert in the form of a defence lawyer either privately or through the legal aid scheme. In theory this should close the gap between the rhetoric of due process and the daily practice of the courts and place the defendant in a position of equality in relation to the police and prosecution. Yet, as I have described in the section, 'Being Represented by a Lawyer under Legal Aid',[32] the mere existence of a defence solicitor or barrister is no guarantee of equality. Indeed, the lawyer's presence may give rise to further contradictions between formality and reality. To begin with, where the defendant cannot afford a lawyer, he must apply to the court for a legal aid order. For these defendants being represented is more of a privilege than a right and it is this initial impression that they are in a privileged position which tends to characterise the subsequent relationship between lawyer and client. The client often does not instruct the lawyer in any meaningful sense of the word; it is rather the lawyer who instructs the client. The lawyer takes down those facts that he considers relevant to the client's case; he tells him how to plead; he decides what aspects of the defendant's character and background to emphasise before the magistrates, whether to challenge the police or probation officer and what sentence to propose to the court. In most cases it is quite clear that it is the lawyer who is in charge. Defendants tend to follow advice and obey instructions.[33] Moreover, the conditions within which many lawyers operate are such as to ensure that the service they offer their clients does not in any way provide the defendant with the power and the knowledge to challenge the legal machinery which is set to convict and punish him.

This does not mean that lawyers do not try to serve their clients' interests, but that their perception of these interests is conditioned by the institutional structure of rewards and sanctions. While obtaining good results in terms of favourable bail decisions and lenient sentences is clearly desirable for defence lawyers, for it enhances their reputation among clients and their standing in the courthouse community, equally important to many of them are the profit margins on each case, the maintenance of good relationships with other courtroom regulars and putting on a good performance in the courtroom. This often means avoiding situations which are likely to be unprofitable or which may potentially threaten the delicate equilibrium of the network of interpersonal relationships which sustains the system. Translated into practical strategies, this in turn may mean staying clear of police stations, ensuring that one's client does not make trouble in court and trying, wherever possible, to find solutions through compromise rather than conflict. The lawyer's role in these circumstances becomes, as one author has described it, that of 'agent-mediator',[34] furthering the institutional aims of the criminal justice system and the class aims of a power elite, while at the same time claiming at a rhetorical level to be the champion of his client.

The probation officer's role, according to this interpretation, is equally contradictory. At one level he is a social worker using the language and techniques of a helping and caring profession in an attempt to meet the needs of defendants and to assist them in overcoming the problems that have caused their conflict with the law. Yet this task may also be seen as promoting through a mixture of coercion and consent the dominant interests of the ruling class. 'The whole notion of rehabilitation involves', according to one writer, 'trying to induce convicted persons to accept and adopt to the existing social system.'[35] In preparing his social enquiry report for the court, for example, probation officers are put in a position where they must either portray the defendant as in some way pathological and therefore in the need of 'help' or they must acknowledge his normality or their own inability to help him and so hand him over to the court for punishment. In attempting to protect individual defendants from the rigours of the penal system, therefore, they must assert their client's abnormality and in doing so affirm the righteousness of the existing social order. It is the defendant who must be changed and not society. This conflict between the rhetoric of rehabilitation and the role probation officers are forced to play within the court system has led recently to some officers refusing to prepare social enquiry reports in cases which they see as political in nature, because they involve defendants who have acted according to strongly held political convictions. Yet, according to this model, the use of probation officers as instruments of repression and control is not confined to these few, isolated cases, but extends throughout the whole range of criminal offences and the whole spectrum of defendants. By operating within a system created by the capitalist state, their humanitarian motives, however sincerely held, become subsumed within the institutional objectives of the system and thus translated into acts which must by their very nature enhance the interests of the ruling class. The only escape from this dilemma is to make themselves effectively impotent agents within the system by, for instance, blaming the failure of society for a defendant's crime and so ensuring that recommendations in the present social enquiry report will be dismissed by the magistrates and that future attempts to influence the court's decisions will fail.

Turning now to the magistrates' decisions, proponents of the power approach would argue that wherever there exists a discretion in the exercise of judicial power, there will be a tendency to discriminate in favour of the dominant classes and against the dominated groups in society. Although there is evidence from the United States showing that black defendants and those on low incomes fare worse than whites and higher income groups in the courts[36] and from Northern Ireland indicating that for some categories of crime Catholics receive heavier sentences than Non-Catholics,[37] there have been no studies published in this country specifically comparing the magistrates' treatment of different groups of defendants. However, it is possible to make certain general observations concerning the exercise of magisterial discretion. For a start, there are certain characteristics which are well known among defence lawyers and probation officers to appeal to a majority of magistrates. These range from features relating to external appearance, such as being smart, clean, beardless and with hair cut short to factors concerning the defendant's standing in the community as evidenced by his job or the wealth and social status of the sureties he is able to present to the court in support of his bail application or of the character witnesses he produces at the sentencing hearing.

Moreover, characteristics associated with a life style reflecting middle-class ideals, regular employment, living with parents, being married, a stable family life, regular employment, association with a traditionally conventional organisation, such as church, youth club or boy scouts, tend to be accepted by the court as positive attributes for bail and sentencing purposes. Characteristics, on the other hand, which appear to run contrary to or to threaten these ideals, such as unemployment, instability in accommodation and in personal relationships, an unconventional manner of dressing or membership of a fringe religious or political group tend to be regarded negatively.

Of course, it is possible to justify such discriminations at the level of formal legal rationality by arguing that the positive attributes are causally related to appearing in court to answer bail and low reconviction rates, while the negative attributes lead to bail-jumping and recidivism. There may be some truth in these justifications, but the fact remains that defendants who are unfortunate enough to come from social backgrounds which do not conform with the magistrates' class-bound conceptions of acceptable life styles run the risk of being dealt with more severely than others, quite irrespective of the seriousness of the offence

with which they are charged. The court, according to this view, therefore serves to reinforce conformity to particular class values and to
sanction behaviour or attitudes which appear to conflict with these
values. Drug cases in the late sixties, where possessors of small amounts
of cannabis were given prison sentences, and the harsh punishments
meted out to black youths convicted of street offences are examples of
the way in which police prosecutorial discretion combined with magisterial discretion over sentencing may operate against specific social
groups whose life styles fail to conform to the class values which the
criminal justice system helps to sustain.[38]

Some writers have suggested that evidence of the class oppression
which, they maintain, characterises the magistrates' courts, may be
found in the reactions of defendants, coming as they do predominantly
from the ranks of the unemployed or low income groups. Certainly,
many defendants find the court atmosphere unpleasant, its rules and
procedures confusing and its decisions unjust. However, few, in my
experience, feel 'a mounting sense of absurdity', as Carlen reports[39] or
adopt a cynical, defeatist approach to the system. The predominant
feelings at least among defendants who plead guilty appear to be ones of
guilt, shame and anxiety. Many more than Carlen suggests apply for a
lawyer to represent them under legal aid[40] and a high proportion of
them say that they are satisfied with the service they receive.[41] The contradictions, absurdities and inequalities which are highlighted by the
power model, while they may exist, appear to escape the notice of most
defendants, or produce no more than non-specific feelings of unfair-
ness, confusion and frustration in them. Perhaps for many defendants
their treatment at the hands of the court regulars is no different than
their treatment at the hands of all other forms of officialdom, be it
education, social security, health or employment. For them, the gaps
between rhetoric and performance, and between formal due process
and informal coercion may characterise so many other aspects of their
lives as to be unremarkable. For them, the predominant concern is
usually to escape as unscathed as possible from the criminal justice
process and to use whatever means are available to them to achieve this
end. This does not necessarily detract from the power model, for it
could well be argued that it is not only within the legal system that the
capitalist state creates the conditions for class dominance, but also in
all other social institutions. However, it does suggest that the model is
one imposed upon the system from outside by people who have chosen
to adopt a particular political and social ideology rather than emerging
spontaneously from the 'victims' of the process.

7. Impressions from the Application of the Process Models

The nature of social theory is such that, except in the limited cases of narrow hypotheses concerning specific facts, it is impossible to prove or disapprove anything — at least in the scientific sense of these terms. The most one can do is to discover whether a particular theory 'fits' the data. Yet, we have seen in this chapter how six different theoretical models may fit at least some of the available data concerning the way magistrates' courts deal with guilty pleaders. The mere, fact that a particular theory may account successfully for some aspects of knowledge concerning a social phenomenon does not bring one closer to the truth in any absolute sense. However, what I have attempted to argue so far in this study is that viewing the social phenomenon from a number of different theoretical vantage points will provide a more 'realistic' account of that phenomenon than would be the case if one limited one's analysis to one or two theoretical approaches or if one denied altogether the relevance of theory in attempting to gain an understanding of the phenomenon in question. The time has now come to consolidate some of the knowledge which we should have gained from the multi-theoretical approach we have undertaken and to ask what advantages there may be in this exercise over more conventional studies of the criminal justice process.

Perhaps the overriding impression that this study will have conveyed to the reader is of the enormous complexity of the operation of even the most simple social system. Even if one deliberately ignores, as we have done, important aspects of the system's operation, it is astonishing how complicated are the interrelationships between the various participants, between the various stages of the process and between the various levels of interaction. This complexity is increased rather than diminished by the use of multiple models, for the same feature within the system may be subject to very different interpretations depending upon the model one is applying. The dock, for example, may be variously interpreted as a necessary courtroom fixture for establishing the accusatorial nature of the proceedings, a symbol of shame and degradation or a device for inhibiting the defendant's participation in the courtroom proceedings and restricting his control over his lawyer.

If multiple versions of what is going on, existing side by side, may legitimately account in different ways for various aspects of the system's operation, it follows that the 'official' version of the workings of magistrates' courts conveyed to students through textbooks[42] and to the general public through the mass communications media, offers only a partial description of these processes. In this official version the concepts of justice conveyed by the formal rules and the conventional wisdoms concerning the roles of police, lawyers, probation officers and magistrates predominate. Yet this version may prove inadequate even to those who are daily involved in operating the system, for, as Carlen has shown, many of the regular participants come to accept alternative definitions, seeing the whole process as a 'game' and the courtroom hearing as a 'performance'.[43] However, even these 'unofficial' accounts may distort or may not fully explain the way in which these actors actually go about their business. Indeed the participants themselves may be unaware of all the norms, expectations, constraints and demands which affect them in their work; or if they are aware of them, they may lack the conceptual framework necessary to convert this awareness into conscious articulation.

Our analysis goes much further than merely casting doubts on the 'official' version of how magistrates' courts work or the descriptions of the participants themselves as to how they operate the system. It also shows up the weakness of *all* explanations which rely on a uni-dimensional approach to the criminal justice system, be it game theory,[44] status passage theory,[45] family theory[46] or theories based upon simple economic or class conflict models of social behaviour. It is a 'game'; it is a 'status passage'; people are trying to maximise their gains and minimise their losses; it is a class-biased system, but it is also much more than all that and to confine one's account of the system's operation to any one of these theoretical approaches is to ignore all other possible explanations and to make the system appear much simpler than it is in fact.

Yet it should not be imagined that this issue merely concerns academic theoreticians. Many theoretical approaches have clear policy objectives which the exponent of the theory may or may not make explicit. They invite the reader not only to take a particular stance towards the phenomenon under observation, but also to urge for changes in the system which will bring it closer to the criteria which the author and the theory consider desirable. Glaser and Strauss point out two aspects of the problem of deriving policies from social theories:

A sociologist often develops a theory that embodies without his realising it his own ideals and the values of his occupation and social class, as well as popular views and myths . . . These witting and unwitting strategies typically result in theories so divorced from the everyday realities of substantive areas that one does not quite know how to apply them, at what part of the social structure to begin applying them, where they fit the data of the substantive area or what the propositions mean in relation to the diverse problems of the area.[47]

These authors appear to assume that providing the theory is sufficiently 'grounded' in data systematically obtained from social research, the problem of subjectivity will automatically be overcome. Yet, as we have seen from our analysis, this is not the case, for it is possible that two or more theories may fit the evidence equally well. Indeed, much of this evidence may itself have come from workers who have applied their own subjective values in choosing what aspects of the system to investigate, what questions to ask and what interpretations to put on the answers they obtained. No matter how many theories we compare or how much evidence we analyse, comparing theories and analysing evidence is not going to bring us any nearer to establishing in any absolute sense what should be the objectives for social policy. These objectives can only come from one's own evocation of the sort of society one wishes to live in. The criteria by which one judges the performance of such social institutions as magistrates' courts will depend upon this overriding model. What then is the relevance, if any, of the foregoing analysis for policy and policy-makers? Apart from the general cautionary lesson it teaches about offering simple solutions based upon a simplistic assessment of the available evidence, a multi-theoretical approach does help to expand the conceptual framework which policy-makers bring with them to the committee room, conference rostrum or parliamentary debate. This is particularly important in legal matters, where the framework has in the recent past been especially narrow and restricted. In addition, placing different theoretical approaches with different policy objectives alongside one another and applying them more or less systematically to the data may spell out more clearly than any other method the limitations of each approach as instruments for policy-making.

Notes

1. See pp. 62-6.
2. See p. 66.
3. See p. 66.
4. See pp. 48-54.
5. See p. 15.
6. See pp. 75-7 and p. 80.
7. See pp. 87-9.

8. See pp. 62–6.

9. See pp. 68–73.

10. See pp. 77–9.

11. See pp. 75–7.

12. See pp. 85–7.

13. See p. 71; pp. 79–81 and p. 85.

14. See pp. 87–8.

15. See p. 65 and p. 76.

16. See p. 78.

17. See p. 78.

18. See p. 80–1.

19. See p. 25.

20. See p. 87.

21. See pp. 87–9.

22. See p. 88.

23. See pp. 88–9.

24. See p. 86.

25. H. Garfinkel, 'Conditions of Successful Degradation Ceremonies', *American Journal of Sociology*, vol. 6 (1956), p. 423.

26. See pp. 40–1.

27. See e.g. A Blumberg, *'Criminal Justice'*, 2nd edn (Quadrangle Books, Chicago, 1970), pp. 104–5.

28. See p. 33.

29. I. Balbus, *The Dialectics of Legal Repression* (Russell Sage Foundation, New York, 1973), p. 5.

30. P. Carlen, *Magistrates' Justice* (Martin Robertson, London, 1976), p. 87.

31. See pp. 165–8 and p. 76.

32. See pp. 68–75.

33. See pp. 74–5.

34. Blumberg, *Criminal Justice*, Ch. 5.

35. J. Garafalo, 'Radical Criminology and Criminal Justice: Points of Divergence and Contact', *Crime and Social Justice*, vol. 10 (1978), pp. 17–25.

36. S. Clarke and G. Koch, 'The influence of Income and Other Factors on Whether Criminal Defendants go to Prison', *Law and Society Review*, vol. 11 (1976), pp. 57–92; M. Woolfgang and M. Riedel, 'Race, Judicial Discretion and the Death Penalty', *The Annals of the American Academy of Political and Social Science*, vol. 407 (1973), p. 118.

37. T. Hadden and P. Hillyard, *Justice in Northern Ireland* (Cobden Trust, London, 1973).

38. See p.

39. Carlen, *Magistrates' Justice*, p. 85.

40. Ibid., p. 83.

41. See note 19, Ch. 4.

42. See e.g. D. Barnard, *The Criminal Court in Action*, 2nd edn (Butterworths, London, 1980); A.K.R. Kirafy, *The English Legal System*, 6th edn (Sweet and Maxwell, London, 1978).

43. Carlen, *Magistrates' Justice*.

44. Blumberg, *Criminal Justice;* Carlen, *Magistrates' Justice*.

45. M. King, 'A Status Passage Analysis of the Defendant's Progress through the Magistrates' Court', *Law and Human Behaviour*, vol. 2, no. 3 (1978), pp. 183–221.

46. J. Griffiths, 'Ideology in Criminal Procedure or A Third Model of the Criminal Process', *The Yale Law Journal*, vol. 79, no. 3 (1970), pp. 359–417.

47. B. Glaser and A. Strauss, *The Discovery of Grounded Theory* (Aldine, Chicago, 1967), p. 47.

Getting the System Right: The Process of Law Reform

In expanding the traditional conceptual framework for our analysis of the criminal justice system, not only have I gone beyond the idealised presentation of the system found in legal textbooks, but I have also tried to place in some sort of social and political context the presentation of criminal justice as a closed system in which duels are fought out between prosecution and defence, between due process and crime control, and between punishment and rehabilitation. The conception of a criminal justice process in such dualistic terms, operating in isolation from everything else that goes on is society, is misleading in two important respects. In the first place it ignores the very real constraints and interests operating upon and within the system that have nothing to do with the establishment of guilt or innocence, the control of crime, the protection of individual rights or the effectiveness of different types of penalty. These constraints and interests may be of a fairly obvious nature, arising from bureaucratic and economic factors, or they may result from the more subtle elusive social elements of power and status. Secondly, the perception of the system as a battleground gives rise to the illusion that real changes can be made simply by altering the rules of combat, be it a shift in the direction of due process, crime control, rehabilitation or retribution. If the last two decades have anything to tell us about the reform of criminal justice it is that changes in the legal rules alone usually change very little in the way the system operates.

The sixties and seventies saw academic lawyers and sociologists joining forces with civil liberties groups and legal practitioners to press for changes in the criminal justice process to make the system fairer, to protect individual rights and to restrain police coercion. Some of the studies I have quoted from in this book were the result of these labours. Indeed, my own work on bail and evidence falls within this liberal reformist tradition. The problem was that we liberal reformists tended to accept at face value the rhetoric of rationality and due process which pervades the formal rules of evidence and procedure. If the system is supposed to be fair and just, and then the existing rules must be enforced and new rules introduced to combat police abuses, help and protect defendants and restrain the excesses of some magistrates. At the same time other (often rather older) legal academics were joining forces with the police and members of the judiciary to take a rather different view of the criminal justice process. If the system is supposed to catch and convict criminals, especially professionall criminals, they asked, why is it that so many of the rules obstruct the police and protect the guilty. This was the view that was expressed by the members of the Criminal Law Revision Committee in its Eleventh Report.[1] This Report was characterised by the belief, in the absence of any real evidence, that the rules were actually having this effect of allowing professional criminals to escape justice and by a general acceptance that changing the rules would alter significally the operation of the system. In the public debate which followed the publication of the Eleventh Report, neither side appear to question the importance of the formal rules as being instrumental both in reflecting how the system operates at present and determining how it should operate in the future once the rules have been changed. It was as if the rules themselves became something symbolic, worth fighting over regardless of what their actual effects might be. Indeed, each side competed with the other to invent far-fetched situations where the existing rules or the proposed changes could lead to gross injustices and manifest absurdities.

During the skirmishes of the last two decades over bail, legal representation, police interrogations and the rules of evidence it was no doubt fondly believed by many within the liberal reformist and police power camps that the government would respond positively to their proposals for changing the system. What in fact happened was that, while some of the liberal reformist proposals did find their way into the statute books, suggestions for strengthening the hands of the police, such as those contained in the Eleventh Report, did not. There is a paradox, however, in the fact that, despite some liberalisation of the law, there was no evidence that the criminal justice system, as practised became more liberal as a direct result of changes in the formal procedural rules, if one takes as measures of liberalisation such things as the treatment of police suspects, the granting of bail, the acquittal rate or an overall reduction in the severity of penalties. On the other hand, despite very little change in the direction of deliberalising these rules, there is absolutely no evidence that the police have been ineffective in their campaigns against organised crime, that a large number of defendants jump bail or that a susbstantial proportion of guilty people are being acquitted by the courts. Yet readers of this book should have no difficulty in explaining this paradox, for they will know that so much of what happens in the criminal justice system in this country depends not on the formal rules, but on the attitudes of decision-makers, on the dealings that take place behind the scenes, out of the reach of the formal rules, and on the institutional pressures and power hierarchy which affect the freedom of action of all participants to the process. They will also know that the only changes in the rules which are likely to have any effect are ones which restrict the discretion of decision-makers, provide resources which are not previously available or withdraw existing resources, make public secret dealings and alter the institutional pressures and power structure. What I now wish to suggest is that governments, meaning the politicians in power and the civil servants who guide them, also know this and that it would be naive to think otherwise. We may recall from our analysis of the courtroom process how it is in the interest of all those involved in the ceremony to give the impression that justice is being done in a rational and neutral manner, regardless of the race, class or political beliefs of the defendant, regardless of the attitudes, social background and political affiliations of the magistrates and regardless of what might have happened behind the walls of the police station, in the corridors outside the courtroom or in the probation officer's office. In just the same way some commentators have suggested that it is in the interests of a government within a liberal state to support the rhetorical notion of neutral and rational justice and the protection of the rights of citizens, while at the same time leaving the way clear for the forces of law and order to repress those who in their view threaten the existing social structure. Moreover, it may also be in the interests of the government to permit those who purvey the social values, which it supports and wishes to impose, to be given an opportunity to express those values in their decision-making. This analogy between the courtroom and the process of reform can be taken further, as we shall see. However, rather than continuing to deal in generalities, it would be appropriate at this stage to look detail at the process of law reform and some examples of the process it action.

1. The Process of Law Reform

Ideally, the process of changing the criminal justice system proceeds in a rational, democratic manner with ample opportunity for all interested parties to air their views and present evidence, for assessment of all the proposals and the evidence supporting them by a neutral advisory body and for the final decision-making to be carried out by the democratically elected representatives of the people. At first glance, the machinery of reform operating in this country would appear to conform with these ideals.

Most reforms to the criminal justice process start with a grievance. Perhaps aspects of the system are working unfairly, are inefficient, have not kept pace with changes in society or advances in technology or make it impossible for certain groups to perform their duties effectively. The original complaints are likely to come from those actively involved in the everyday operation of the system. Policemen, lawyers and probation officers have their own professional or representative groups who undertake the task of representing the views of their members to sympathetic politicians and to government departments involved in the operation of the courts. The complaints are usually accompanied by proposals for reforming the system. There are, however, participants in the criminal justice process who have no professional body or organised lobby to air their grievances and represent their interests. These are the suspects and defendants. Their access to the law reform process lies through civil liberty pressure groups, such as the National Council for Civil Liberties, Justice or Release, through their Member of Parliament or through journalists and researchers who record their grievances and report them to a wider audience.

The second stage in the process of reform is the official enquiry stage. The enquiry might take the form of a Royal Commission or it might be on a smaller scale, for example, a Departmental Committee set up specifically for the purpose of investigating the grievances and proposals for reform or an existing permanent committee, such as the Criminal Law Revision Committee which may turn its attention to the specific matters which are causing disquiet. Whatever form the enquiry may take, the members of the enquiry team are almost invariably selected by the government, either directly, by appointment or by accepting nominations from a number of interested organisations. The government will also almost invariably set out the terms of reference for the enquiry and the subsequent review and recommendations of the enquiry team will be limited by these terms of reference. The committee of enquiry will, after it has reviewed all the available evidence and proposals for reform, draw up a report which will set out its findings and recommendations for changes in the operation of the system. Depending on the status of the enquiry committee, this report will either be presented directly to Parliament for debate or will be considered by the goverment minister and officials in his department before any discussion takes place in Parliament.

The final stage in the law reform process, the submission of proposals to the legislature, comes very close to the ideal suggested earlier. Most legislation concerning criminal justice seems these days to start in the House of Lords. The Bill is first presented for debate at its Second Reading, when anyone in the Chamber may speak on any aspect of the proposals or the background to their introduction. The Bill then proceeds to a Committee Stage when each clause is discussed and, when necessary, voted upon. In the Lords the Committee usually consists of the whole House. There then follows the Report Stage at which the Committee's amendments are debated and usually approved. The final stage is the Fourth Reading, where there may be an opportunity for further debate, before the Bill receives Royal Assent. Having gone through the Lords the same four stages are repeated in the Commons, the only substantial difference being that here the Committee Stage is undertaken by a Standing Committee, which consists of a small group of MPs sitting in the same proportion to their party's representation in the Main Chamber of the House, so that the government will have a majority on Committee. Amendments to the Bill may be presented either at the Committee Stage or at the Report Stage. All amendments, unless withdrawn, must be voted upon by both Chambers of the House before they become part of the Act. Let us now look at two examples of the manner in which the criminal justice process was reformed in recent years. The first concerns the Bail Act of 1976 and the second, two sections of the Criminal Law Act 1977.

2. The Bail Act 1976

The complaints which led eventually to the presentation of the Bail Bill before Parliament came from diverse sources and concerned many different aspects of the bail system. A number of academic researchers had produced reports suggesting that a large number of defendants were remanded in custody unnecessarily, because magistrates had insufficient information about them other than that which came from the police and, therefore, tended to follow blindly police recommendations.[2] Research reports had also shown that defendants were often unpresented when magistrates remanded them in custody and that they said very little in support of their applications for bail. Legal aid was not available for appeals to a judge in chambers against refusal of bail. Furthermore, there had been complaints about the way in which the police used their control over bail both from the police station and magistrates' court in threats or promises to the defendant in order to get him to confess. There had, moreover, been reports in the newspapers and on television about the unsatisfactory conditions at local prisons and remand centres, where prisoners awaiting trial were often made to spend 23 hours a day in overcrowded cells. On top of all this, the Official Statistics revealed the disturbing fact that as many as half of those defendants who had been remanded in custody before being sentenced eventually walked out of the court with a non-custodial sentence or having been acquitted altogether. For those acquitted there was not even a right to compensation.

The Labour Government's response to these grievances was twofold. First, the Home Office Research Unit embarked upon a study of the effects of those sections of the Criminal Justice Act 1967 which had been passed with the intention of reducing the number of defendants remanded in custody. Secondly, it seized upon a proposal from the Magistrates' Association in 1971 to set up a Home Office Working Party. Two significant points about this Working Party were, first, its terms of reference and, secondly, its membership.

The terms of reference read: 'To review practice and procedure in Magistrates' Courts relating to the grant and refusal of bail and to make recommendations.'[3] Thus any consideration of matters which did not relate to what went on in the courtroom were excluded right from the start. The issues were in effect narrowed down to questions concerning the criteria for granting or refusing bail and the procedure governing bail applications. What had started out as a number of wide-ranging social problems involving fundamental aspects of the criminal justice and penal systems had been reduced to questions for lawyers and those involved in the administration of the law. Having thus defined the nature of the problem, it was perhaps not surprising that invitations to investigate the problem went out from the Home Office to a number of official bodies concerned in the administration of justice who were asked to propose members for the Working Party. These bodies included the Association of Chief Police Officers, London Magistrates' Clerks Assoocia-tion, the Magistrates' Association and the Justices' Clerks Society. The remaining members, including the Chairman, came from the Home Office itself as did the Secretary. It was not simply that all these bodies were involved in bail applications at magistrates' courts, but that to-gether they represented the power nexus within these courts. Those who had no power over decision-making, the defendants and their lawyers, were invited, through organisations representing their interests, to sub-mit written and oral evidence. The arrangement was in effect an approximation to the courtroom situation with counsel for the defence presenting the evidence for assessment by the magistrates and their clerks. The only difference was that on the Working Party the magistrates and clerks were joined by the police and Home Office representatives. The courtroom prosecutors had joined forces with the judicial assessors. From what I recall as a member for the NCCL/Cobden Trust delegation giving evidence before the Working Party, the actual proceedings were not so dissimilar from those of a criminal court. I even remember being cross-examined and asked trick questions by one of the police officers on the Working Party.

It was no surprise that the Working Party's Report, published in 1974, while recommending a change of attitude in the granting of bail, proposed no spectacular reforms in the bail system in magistrates' courts. There should be no alteration, for example, in the three established reasons for refusing bail and no attempt to define the circumstances in which bail should be granted. There should be a presumption in favour of bail, but couched in general terms only. Sureties should be retained and an offence of absconding should be introduced in place of personal recognizances. Magistrates should be required to give reasons when they refused bail. All these reforms were described by one commentator as 'lawyers' law'[4] in the sense that they would change the law in the statute book without having any real impact on the decision-making process.

In a rare excursion beyond their terms of reference the Working Party revealed something of the preconceptions with which they tackled their task. They stated that in their view the law which allowed a senior police officer to refuse bail from a police station on the sole ground that he considered the case to be 'a serious one' contained 'adequate safeguards' and needed no change.[5] Elsewhere in their Report they rejected the Cobden Trust's proposal that, as in a number of American courts, a points-score system based on a defendant's roots in the community should be used to provide a recommendation to magistrates on whether or not that defendant should be released on bail. This proposal, according to the Working Party, was unacceptable, because it 'might be seen by magistrates as interfering with their judicial discretion'.[6]

Yet it would be a mistake to give the impression that the Report made no proposals which, had they been accepted, could have had a real impact on the criminal justice system. The Working Party did, for example, call for more bail hostels to be provided, which could have prevented detaining defendants under grim conditions in prisons and remand centres simply because they had nowhere to live. They also

suggested the introduction of information forms, which would have
ensured that before it made a bail or custody decision every bench of
magistrates would have before it some basic information about the
defendant's employment record, his accommodation and his family ties.
Moreover, the Working Party's proposal that court staff should complete these forms would have had the effect of breaking the police
monopoly over the information process in those cases where the defendant was unrepresented. From the government's point of view, however,
both these proposals suffered from the same fatal flaw — they would
have cost money.

Two government initiatives resulted directly from the publication of
the Home Office Working Party's Report. The first was a Home Office
circular on bail procedure distributed to magistrates' clerks, the police
and probation officers in October 1975.[7] The second was the publication of the Bail Bill and its introduction in the House of Lords early in
1976. The basic contents of these two documents were very similar,
except that in addition to suggesting changes in the criteria and procedure for deciding bail applications, the Home Office circular drew
attention to the Working Party's recommendation that standard procedures should be devised for providing courts with information about
the defendant's community ties. It then added: 'The Secretary of State
would accordingly be grateful if courts would now consider the introduction of schemes along the lines described, within existing resources.'
According to a parliamentary Written Answer given in the House of
Lords on 28 February 1980 to a question tabled by Lord Donaldson,
only 36 courts out of a possible 680 had made any attempt to earn the
gratitude of the Secretary of State, apart from Camberwell Green,
where the Vera Institute had already set up its pilot project for the use of
information forms. Of these new schemes, twelve, it appears, are operated by the police.

The Bail Bill was not one of those Parliament Bills which fire the
imagination either of politicians or the public at large. As far as the
majority of politicians were concerned, being a measure which concerned the administration of justice, it was better left to lawyers, for in
the words of Lord Wigoder during the Second Reading of the Bill,
'there has never been any votes in penal reform'.[8] It was not particularly
surprising, therefore, that with one or two notable exceptions, the
principal speakers in the Lords and Commons were lawyers,
magistrates, judges and the representative of the Police Federation.
Unsurprising also, in view of the backgrounds and affiliations of
most of the speakers, was the fact that the debate proceeded in the

main on the basis of unchallenged assumptions about the administrators of justice. The integrity of the police was, according to one member of the Lords, such that the courts are able 'to feel that they can, with confidence in the great majority of cases rely on what is being said to them'.[9] 'Magistrates will not fail to do their proper duty',[10] 'apply their discretion reasonably and in a responsible manner',[11] and 'do the best they can in every case that comes before them'[12] — sentiments that suggested that the speakers had not even taken the trouble to read the reports of the Cobden Trust or Home Office Research Unit and their criticisms of the handling of bail decisions by magistrates and the police.

A further unchallenged assumption which punctuated the debates was that no resources were available to improve the existing bail system, either for information verification schemes, or for the relief of the overcrowded conditions in remand prison, or to provide more bail hostels. The 'present financial conditions' and 'severe restrictions on public expenditure' were two phrases which sprang readily from the lips of government spokesmen, this at a time when, for example, literally millions of pounds were being thrown away on a totally useless sea blockade on the Mozambique port of Beira.

Only in the debate following the Commons Second Reading did the parliamentary discussion briefly penetrate the barrier of complacency and look behind the bland facade of magistrates' courts as places where everyone is striving to do justice and to protect the rights of individuals. Significantly, the MP who drew attention to the deliberate injustices in the system was John Stonehouse, who was himself at that time facing serious fraud charges, and had suffered a period in custody awaiting trial. He told the Commons that:

> Unfortunately the police . . . still take the view . . . that denial of bail is a useful weapon in their pursuance of an individual whom they wish to make a convict. The police, after all, have regarded themselves as having a duty to get convictions. It is not part of their responsibility to try to see the defendant's point of view. The police identify a person whom they consider to be a criminal and their efforts are directed towards obtaining a conviction . . . The police have an interest in denying bail to a defendant. They are not interested in bringing before the court the full facts.[13]

However, Mr Stonehouse's speech made no discernible impact on the debate. No one even bothered to reply to the view he had put forward, perhaps because Stonehouse, like defendants in magistrates' courts, was already a discredited person, so there was no need to take him seriously.

The notion that refusal of bail might actually help crime control was tentatively suggested by Mr Eldon Griffiths who spoke of an 'imbalance between the human misery created by crime and the way in which the offender is dealt with by being bailed, under-sentenced or paroled too early'.[14] And Mr Andrew Bennett reported that some policemen in his constituency believed that 'a little time in prison is good for some people'.[15] In general, the Second Reading debate provided an open forum for MPs to give vent to their particular criticism of the criminal justice system. The conditions in remand prisons, especially Brixton, were roundly condemned;[16] compensation was proposed for defendants acquitted after suffering a period in custody; suggestions for speeding up the criminal justice process were put forward;[17] the idea that judges should visit prisons to hear appeals against refusal of bail was mooted and sympathy was expressed for the deprivations suffered by defendants held in custody and their families.[18] Yet none of these speeches appeared to have the slightest impact on the outcome of the debate or on the contents of the Bail Act eventually approved by Parliament.

At the Committee Stage where the serious business of examining bills in detail is undertaken, the only substantial change to the original Bail Bill presented to the Lords was an extension agreed by the government of the presumption in favour of bail to cover convicted but unsentenced defendants. All the other proposed amendments were either withdrawn or defeated on a vote. In fact, excluding the government's own amendment there were only two divisions, abortive attempts by the Labour MP, Mr Robert Kilroy-Silk, to repeal the new offence of absconding and to restrict the police discretion over refusal of bail. An inordinate amount of time was spent by the Committee in debating the wording of the criterion for refusing bail which Lord Hailsham had succeeded in having amended during the Lords stage. Should the test be on the basis of *'probable grounds for believing'* (that the defendant would fail to surrender to custody, etc.) or should there be an *'unacceptable risk'*. The formula eventually adopted was *'substantial grounds for believing'*. The effects in practice of such subtle variations in the wording are difficult to predict, but one would guess that Baroness Ward, herself a magistrate, was right when she told the Lords: 'Do you think that magistrates get very excited about words; they certainly do not.'[19]

But perhaps the most revealing comments on the Bail Bill and its likely effects came from Mr Ivan Lawrence. He first told the Commons at the Second Reading:

> I do not welcome the Bill. I do not welcome any legislation which will
> not remedy positive evil or do positive good. We spend too much of
> our time churning out legislation which will not achieve very much.[20]

At the Report Stage he elaborated on this view:

> . . . Fourteen years of making almost weekly applications for bail on
> behalf of countless clients has led me not to see much sense in the
> Bill . . . What is wrong with our penal system is not so much that too
> many people are unjustly remanded in custody but that the Govern-
> ment and perhaps successive governments have totally failed to pro-
> vide an adequate penal system with adequate prison accommo-
> dation for those who are properly sentenced . . .
>
> Secondly, I believe that people outside this House may regard the
> Bill as a measure aimed at bringing about a substantial change in the
> operation of the law. They may take the view that it liberalizes the
> situation or that if further weakens the forces of law and order —
> and in some respects it may possibly do so in limiting the discretion of
> the judiciary — but broadly those beliefs would, I think, be wrong.
> The process of the courts, granting and refusing bail, will continue
> very much as it has always done, through the exercise of broad prin-
> ciples of common sense and good will by all parties to the operation of
> our legal system.[21]

What general comments may one draw about the process of reform
from this example? An important point is the way in which it illustrates
how government is able to keep firm control over the process of reform
and the eventual legislative changes which find their way into the Statute Book. In the case of the Bail Act this was achieved by several
devices. In the first place it was the government who chose the format
for the committee of enquiry — a Home Office Working Party — and
decided upon the terms of reference and which organisations should be
invited to nominate members. It would appear that even at this early
stage the intention of the government was to do nothing which would
involve any substantial increase in expenditure on crminal justice or
which would in any way offend the administrators of the system, police,
justices' clerks or magistrates. Secondly, the government was able to
deflect those proposals of the Working Party which would have cost
money, such as the proposal for bail hostels, for additional court staff to
complete bail information sheets or for legal aid to be available for

appeals to judge in chambers by making recommendations to the court and to the police in the form of a memorandum and deliberately excluding them from legislation which was confined to changes in procedure and criteria. A cynical interpretation of the government's objectives in promoting the Bail Bill was that it wished to give the impression that important changes were being made to the criminal justice process and so silence the critics of magistrates' courts and the manner in which these courts handled bail-custody decisions. At the same time, it is clear that the government was extremely anxious that none of the statutory changes should involve it in any additional expenditure or in any substantial way diminish the powers and discretion which the police and magistrates exercised over the system. What emerged at the end of the law reform process appears to support this cynical interpretation. The government's response to the widespread and serious complaints over the operation of the bail system and the treatment of remand prisoners was, as we have seen, a series of changes which in fact changed very little.

The official statistics[22] give little support to any claims that the Bail Act itself has had a significant impact on the decisions of magistrates and judges. Admittedly, there has been a fall in the proportion of unsentenced defendants remanded in custody both before and after conviction between 1975 and 1978, but the major reduction in these figures is attributable to the Home Office circular of 1975 and not to the introduction of the Bail Act in 1976. It is also interesting to note that, according to the authors of the 1978 Prison Department Statistics, the most important factor in the reduction of the number of young offenders remanded in custody was not the Bail Act, but an order made under the Children and Young Persons Act 1969 passed in August 1977, which 'laid down more stringent conditions before a person aged between 14 and 16 can be remanded to a prison . . .' (p. 22) introducing, in other words, restrictions on magisterial discretion which are conspicuously absent from the provisions of the Bail Act.

Furthermore, the proportion of defendants who do not receive a custodial sentence on remand has dropped only marginally since the introduction of the Bail Act and still stands at around 44 per cent suggesting that many defendants continue to be remanded in custody unneccessarily by judges and magistrates.

3. The Criminal Law Act 1977

Rather than examining in detail all the different changes in the criminal justice system brought about by this Act, I have selected two of its provisions, which, I believe, illustrate directly contrasting patterns of law reform. These are, (1) the conversion of assaults against the police from a hybrid offence into one triable at magistrates' courts and (2) the right of a person in police custody to have someone informed of his whereabouts. The first of these changes was a government proposal contained in the Criminal Law Bill, while the second was inserted in defiance of the government as the result of an initiative by a private member at the Report Stage. Let us examine each of these provisions in turn.

Assaults Against the Police

In 1973 the government set up an interdepartmental committee (Home Department and Lord Chancellor's Department) under the Chairmanship of Lord Justice James. The purpose of the committee was 'To determine what distribution of criminal business between the Crown Court and Magistrates' Court is most consistent with the interests of justice.'[23] Despite the Beeching streamlining of the Crown Court there had been serious congestion resulting in long delays for defendants awaiting trial and this had given rise to questions in Parliament and to concern amongst the judiciary and legal profession. Furthermore, Crown Court cases are extremely costly to the state, involving not only the payment of the judge's salary and the fees of the lawyers, but also the expenses and loss of earnings of the jury. It was, therefore, in the government's interests to try to reduce the number of cases that went for trial to the Crown Court. Unlike the Bail Working Party, the James Committee had no police representative among its members, but it did include, as well as the expected sprinkling of judges and magistrates, two academic lawyers, a barrister and a solicitor specialising in criminal work. In addition to the evidence taken from interest groups, the Committee also had before it the results of a Social Survey commissioned by the government on the attitudes of defendants towards the magistrates' courts and the Crown Courts. This survey, published in 1976 provided little in the way of justification for depriving defendants of their right to a jury trial. Its author, commenting on the results of the survey, wrote,

> The outstanding feature is the considerable proportion of defendants . . . who were critical of magistrates' impartiality. Even among those who chose to be tried by magistrates and whose cases were disposed of by the lower court fifty-one percent agreed strongly that magistrates paid more attention to what the police said than to

what they said.[24]

> . . . The fact that over two-thirds of the two groups who chose to appear before magistrates believe that there is a bias toward the police must be a cause for concern.

Although these results had not then been published, the James Committee had them before it came to consider the status of assaults on the police. At that time the offence was 'hybrid'. It could be tried either before magistrates or before a jury in the Crown Court, but it was up to the prosecution, not the defence, to select the place of trial. In practice, however, the hybrid nature of the offence did allow defendants who were charged with assaulting a police officer in addition to other offences (a not uncommon occurrence, since many alleged assaults against the police take place during arrest for another offence) to have the matter heard before a jury. The James Committee in its Report was adamant that the possibility of jury trial should be extended to a positive right.

> In our view the present position, whereby in effect the prosecution can choose to take the case on indictment but the defendant has no choice, is indefensible. Where the case is contested there is often a straight conflict between the evidence of the defendant and that of the police; if there is such a conflict, it can be said that the prosecution has a special involvement in the case and that therefore it is particularly suitable for resolution by a jury. If the offence is retained, we recommend that it should carry a right to trial by jury unless the maximum penalties are severely curtailed.[25]

Yet the publication of the Criminal Law Bill, far from giving the defendant the right to jury trial, reduced assaults against the police to the status of a summary offence, that is one triable only before a magistrates' court. The issue was first raised in Parliament at the House of Lords Committee Stage when Viscount Dilhorne and later Lord Gifford attempted to remove this offence from the list of those to be tried by summary trial only. Two major arguments were put forward for retaining the existing hybrid status of the offence. The first was that assaults against the police were serious matters, both in terms of the seriousness with which society regarded them and in terms of the consequences to the defendant. Lord Gifford pointed out that, 'Magistrates commonly (and in view of the severity of the offence, often rightly) impose immediate sentences of imprisonment upon people of good character . . . '[26] — an observation which he backed up with some statistical evidence. The second argument was that magistrates were biased in favour of the police to the extent that, according to Lord Gifford's experience as a barrister, even where a policeman's injuries justified such serious charges as assault occasioning actual or grievous bodily harm, the police chose the lesser offence of assaulting a police officer, simply to keep the matter in the magistrates' court, where they were confident of obtaining a conviction, since the magistrates were inclined to believe a policeman's evidence rather than that of a defendant.[27] A third argument, incorporating the other two, was that the government had flown directly in the face of the James Committee's recommendations that there should be a right to jury trial in such cases.

Lord Harris, for the government, then produced statistics which, he claimed, showed that, contrary to Lord Gifford's assertions, magistrates were more likely than juries to acquit in cases of assault against the police. In 1975 27 per cent of the 1,457 contested cases before magistrates had resulted in acquittals as opposed to only 20 per cent of the 225 contested cases in the Crown Court.[28] Lord Gifford, however, argued that these figures did not compare like with like since, as the choice of venue was up to the prosecution, one might expect the police to bring before the Crown Court only those cases which they believed to have a strong chance of success, prefering to leave weaker cases for the magistrates to decide.[29]

Nevertheless, Lord Harris went on to argue that had the James Committee seen these statistics it might well have come to different conclusions concerning the status of assaults against the police. A further reason for not implementing the James Committee's recommendation was added in the Commons by the government spokesman, Mr Brynmore John at the Committee Stage, when he pointed out that the James Committee's proposal had ben qualified by 'the very pregnant phrase . . . "unless the maximum penalties are severely curtailed" '.[30] The Bill did reduce the penalties from a maximum of two years' imprisonment and an unlimited fine to six months' imprisonment plus a fine of £1,000. 'We took the view', he added, 'that there was a significant reduction as to entitle us to take the other course without breaking the spirit of the James Report.' This argument, however, did not impress Alex Lyon, a former Home Officer Minister, who stated that:

> The offence is triable on the whole at the present time in the Magistrates' Court, and what the Government have done is to say that the

maximum penalty which the magistrates can impose is the maximum in any event, because they can only impose six months imprisonment. Therefore there never really was any particular diminution in the sentences which would be the maximum in the average case. The Government have gone against the recommendations of the James Committee.[31]

The suggestion in the Lords that the police might be unhappy with the change which the government proposed led Lord Harris to reveal that both the Police Federation and the Association of Chief Police Officers had 'expressed themselves in support of the Government's position on this matter'.[32] This was perhaps surprising in view of the fact that the maximum penalties were being reduced. Indeed, Mr Kilroy-Silk saw the police support of the change as evidence that magistrates discriminated in their favour. 'No other organisation or individual of any substance', he argued, 'seems to be particularly attached to the idea that these cases must be tried solely by magistrates, and one naturally wonders why the police prefer to resist what is now proposed in this amendment and took such a strong line with the Home Office and in evidence to the James Committee.'[33]

However, despite the evidence from the government's own Social Survey, the strongly worded recommendation of the James Committee, amendments proposed in both Houses of Parliament and a range of arguments directed against the change in the status of the offence, the government none the less carried the day and assaults against the police became an offence triable only in a magistrates' court.

It is worth mentioning that the other major recommendation of the James Committee which failed to win the approval of the Commons was that making thefts of under £20 triable only by a magistrates' court. Although originally included in the Criminal Law Bill, this proposal was withdrawn in the House of Lords, the government offering very little in the way of resistance. It is perhaps significant that the police appeared to have had no strong views on this issue, the main argument against the withdrawal of the right to jury trial being the effects of conviction on the reputation and job prospects of defendants.

The Right to have Someone Informed when Arrested

During the Commons Committee Stage of the Criminal Law Bill, Mr Alex Lyon put down an amendment to make it mandatory for a solicitor to have access to a client who is being detained for questioning or who has been arrested. In the discussion that followed it became clear that some members of the House knew very well what went on behind the walls of police stations. 'We all know', said Mr Nicholas Fairbairn, 'that the police have and use techniques to obtain the additional necessary evidence which oral statements may provide and which eventually bring people to justice.'[34] Mr Mark Carlisle, a former Home Office Minister, added that 'clearly, at times, the police put pressure on people to make confessions. Where I think they do a disservice is in denying that it happens and therefore lending an air of scepticism to the evidence.'[35] 'It seems to me', said Mr Edward Lyons, 'that the balance is in favour of the police up to the time that an accused man leaves the police-station.'[36] However the government in the person of Mr Brynmore John was able to stave off any vote on the issue by drawing the Committee's attention to the fact that the recently-appointed Royal Commission on Criminal Procedure would shortly be considering the whole area.

When Mr Alex Lyon withdraw his motion, the last thing the Home Secretary, Mr Rees and his Home Office colleagues could have expected was that the whole issue of a suspect's rights in police detention would be raised again at the Report Stage. Yet Mr George Cunningham had put down for debate a new clause which read:

> Where any person has been arrested, other than under the Prevention of Terrorism Act 1976, and is being held in custody in a police station or other premises, he shall be entitled to have information of his arrest and of the place where he is being held sent to a person of his choosing.[37]

Moreover, Mr Rees and his colleagues could hardly have anticipated that a clause put down at this late stage, unsupported by the government, would be likely to receive much encouragement from MPs. It must have come as something of a surprise to the Home Secretary, therefore, when MP after MP rose from both sides of the House to give accounts of cases they knew where the police had, seemingly without justification, held suspects incommunicado.

Mr Ian Mikardo: I wish to quote two cases within my constituency experience. One is that of a boy of sixteen who was picked up by the police on his way from work, which would have been at about 5.0 p.m. or 6.0 p.m. His parents did not know where he was until two o'clock in the morning . . . His mum was very worried about him and rang all the local hospitals. Can that be right?

The second case is an even more glaring one. It is that of a woman who was taken to a police-station and asked if she could telephone her husband at his place of work so that he might leave work, go home and let the kids into the flat when they came home from school and give them something to eat. She was told 'No. You cannot.' Can this be right?[38]

Mr Rees-Davies: Where the police are arresting people of known bad character, it is becoming a practice rather than a rule not only to take them into custody but not to allow them to communicate at all for a very substantial period of time, even as long as forty-eight hours.[39]

Mr Christopher Price: Colin Jackson was held for well over twenty-four hours after his arrest. His repeated requests to tell his mother and father — he is only sixteen — were refused. . .finally he was brought into court without his mother and father being informed as to where he was.[40]

Mr Frank Hooley: . . . a young West Indian boy [who] took his girlfriend home one Saturday night. After leaving her he was standing at the bus stop waiting to go home when he was pounced upon by the police who claimed that he had been involved in a series of burglaries. He was carted off to the police-station and interrogated, and then taken to another police-station where he was kept for several hours. The police went to his home and searched it without a warrant. They made no attempt to contact his parents or to allow him to do so. In the event, someone else was arrested for the crimes and that young man was acquitted.[41]

Mr Graham Page: . . . We have all received complaints from constituents whose relatives have been arrested and who have been unable to communicate with their families. We should put that situation right.[42]

Mr Merlyn Rees, the Home Secretary, was clearly taken aback by this response. His rather floundering speech against the proposed new clause did just what the proposer of the motion, Mr Cunningham, anticipated. It invoked the Royal Commission on Criminal Procedure which, he stated, 'will take some time, but it is most important that we should look at the matter in depth and that the wider aspects should be considered'.[43] Mr Rees then told the House that he had no reason to believe 'that there is an overwhelming number of cases in which people are held incommunicado'.[44] If there were a 'number of cases' then this was obviously a matter to which he should put his mind. However the new clause, as it was drawn, would create difficulties for police investigation and, moreover, gave no clear indication as to what would happen if the provision was not observed.[45] The Home Secretary believed that a statutory provision was not the right way of dealing with the matter and, in a final attempt to prevent the amendment from proceeding, he promised to find a way of bringing proposals before the House. However, when pressed by MPs, he replied that he was not able to give a commitment to a firm time-scale for these new proposals. Although this vague undertaking succeeded in winning over some of the MPs present, including Sir Michael Havers, the Opposition spokesman, it failed to forestall the amendment. The new clause was passed by 89 votes to 86.

Just over a week later the government brought the amendment before the House of Lords, having in the interim, it appears, received strong representations from the Association of Chief Police Officers.[46] Lord Harris gave the Lords examples of the way in which the clause, if allowed to remain unchanged, could seriously hamper the police in their fight against crime.

> The police may be dealing with a gang rape. They may have arrested one of the gang but not others. If early news of his arrest leaks out to the other members of the gang they may escape, and it might prove much more difficult to bring them before the courts.[47]

Government amendments were, therefore, proposed to meet the police objection. The right of a person to have 'intimation of his arrest sent to a *person of his choosing*' was changed to '*a person reasonably named*'. More significantly, a qualification was added to the provision allowing the police to delay in informing someone of the arrest, '*where some delay is necessary in the interests of justice or prevention of crime or the apprehension of offenders*'. As a palliative the government included within the scope of the provision people arrested under the Prevention of Terrorism Act 1976 and added the words '*without delay*', which Mr Cunningham had claimed in the Commons had been mistakenly left out of his original motion. So the new clause as amended by the government now read:

> Where any person has been arrested and is being held in custody in a police-station or other premises, he shall be entitled to have

intimation of his arrest and of the place where he is being held sent
to one person reasonably named by him, without delay or, where
some delay is necessary in the interest of the investigation or prevention of crime or the apprehension of offenders, with no more delay
than is so necessary.

The amended clause passed through the Lords without a hitch, only
three members, apart from Lord Harris, making any comment.

At the Commons, however, it had a somewhat rougher ride. Mr
Bruce Douglas Mann pointed out that:

> The clause we have now provides no real protection, because in
> every case where the police wish to have a reason to refuse they can
> always say that the provisions in the clause are applicable.[48]

Moreover, according to Mr Christopher Price,

> It puts us back to square one regarding the behaviour of the police
> giving a carte blanche to the police that they already possess in the
> Judges' Rules to decide on the spot to deny the right of information
> to a relative.[49]

The Home Secretary assured the House that the workings of the new
provision would be carefully monitored and that a Home Office circular would be issued advising the police on how they should put the
new law into effect. Mr Alex Lyon, however, was not convinced by
these assurances. He told the House that a previous circular to the
police on the issue of access to lawyers under the Judges' Rules had
done 'a fat lot of good'. 'Even if the provision is contained in legislation',
he argued, 'it will not change the situation.'[50] There was a much fuller
House than for the original debate on the new clause, perhaps because
the government was anxious that its amendments should not be rejected. In any event, this time the government achieved an overwhelming majority of 174.

What are we to make of the way these two proposals for reform
fared in the hands of the politicians and their advisers? In the first
place, both these proposed reforms represented important changes in
the process. Unlike most of the proposals in the Bail Bill, they were
not mere paper reforms. Giving the defendant the choice of a jury
trial in a charge of assault against the police would undoubtedly have
resulted in a substantial increase in the number of cases before the

Crown Court and, knowing the difference in attitude towards the police between magistrates and juries, one can have little doubt that the number of acquittals could also have risen dramatically. This possibility was not, I suggest, entirely ignored by the Police Federation and Association of Chief Police Officers when they advised both the James Committee and the Home Office to make the offence triable only at the magistrates' court. On the face of things it does seem extraordinary that the two organisations whose consistent clamour in recent years has been for tougher sentences and greater protection for police officers should have lent their support to a provision which lowered the maximum penalty for attacking a policeman. One can only surmise that the certainty of conviction was more attractive to these police organisations than the possibility of harsher sentences.

The reform of providing a suspect with the right to have someone informed of his arrest, as originally proposed, would also have had serious repercussions for the operation of the criminal justice system. It would have represented a very real threat to police techniques of interrogation, which, as we have seen, rely to a considerable extent upon the ability to isolate the suspect and prevent any communication between him and the outside world. The presence of solicitors at police stations in large numbers all pressing for access to their clients could well have presented serious problems for the police. Moreover, the mere knowledge that someone outside was aware of his arrest and detention at the police station might have made some suspects that much more resistent to police pressures to confess. It would appear, however, from Lord Harris's speech to the House of Lords that the Association of Chief Police Officers' objections to this reform rested on the fear that the suspect in police custody might warn his criminal associates and so enable them to escape arrest. This particular problem could easily have been overcome by framing the law so as to deny the suspect the right to inform, where the police had reasonable grounds for believing that there were other people involved in the commission of the offence and that these others were still at large. Instead, the Home Office, presumably with the advice of the police, chose a formula which gave police officers a broad discretion to delay giving out information of the arrest and at the same time made it almost impossible for anyone to accuse the police of abusing this discretion. In other words, the government succeeded in effectively neutralising the original proposal, turning it into a paper, rather than a real, reform.

A second important lesson to be learnt from these reforms is the extent which the Home Office and police operate as a team to thwart any threat to the existing structure of the criminal justice system. The fact that the Home Office is the government department responsible for the police does not in itself offer a satisfactory explanation as to why ministers and officials in that department take it upon themselves to seek the views of the Police Federation and Association of Chief Police Officers whenever an issue arises which might affect their interests. The Home Office is also responsible for the protection of individuals against policemen who abuse their powers, but one has yet to see it consult with civil liberties organisations about the form and content of impending legislation. This special relationship between the police and Home Office has the effect of ensuring that the police view will almost invariably prevail even when, as in the case of the James Committee Report, an independent body has previously rejected that view.

This leads to a third important point, which concerns committees of enquiry. It has long been recognised that when a government finds itself under pressure a useful delaying tactic is to appoint a Royal Commission or some other committee of enquiry to look into the situation. Subsequently, whenever an MP attempts to raise matters which might fall within the Committee's remit, the government spokesman will refer the MP to the Committee's existence and tell him that any changes must await the report of its findings. Indeed, the Home Secretary, Mr Merlyn Rees, used just this strategy in his attempt to forestall the introduction of the clause giving arrested persons the right to have someone informed. He told the House of Commons that:

> The Prime Minister has set up a Royal Commission to look into the prosecuting process. There will be wide consideration that will take some time, but it is most important that one should look at the matter in depth and that the wider aspects should be considered.[51]

We have also seen how, once it has decided upon the strategy of setting up a committee of enquiry, the government is able to influence the final report of the Committee by careful selection of the chairman and members and by setting the terms of reference in such a way as to pre-empt any embarrassment to the government. What the experience of the James Committee and the subsequent Criminal Law Bill have taught us is the way the government, even the same government responsible for setting up the Committee, was able, where expedient, virtually to ignore the Committee's recommendation and even to make changes which flew in the face of that recommendation. It is perhaps surprising that, despite these lessons, there are still many people and several organisations concerned with the reform of the criminal law and its administration who pin their faith on Royal Commissions and committees of enquiry as a method of achieving their objectives.

A final matter arising from the Criminal Law Bill reforms which requires some comment is the role of the House of Lords. It would appear to be no coincidence that both Bills we have discussed began their parliamentary life in the Lords and that by the time they reached the elected representatives of the people, in the Commons, they had already had stamped on them a Lords' seal of approval. On matters concerning criminal justice the House of Lords, consisting as it does of hereditary peers, elder statesmen and the favourites of past prime ministers, is notoriously conservative. Thus even when the government was caught off its guard at the Commons Report Stage by the introduction of a new clause which threatened police powers, it was none the less able by making use of the House of Lords effectively to take the sting out of the new clause, even after the democratically elected representatives of the people had voted in favour of the original provisions.

4. Conclusions

In the preceding pages I have hinted on a number of occasions at the similarities and connections between the administration of justice by the police and criminal courts and the machinery for monitoring and reforming the criminal justice system. Of course, the usual approach is to treat the police and the courts as separate and independent from the committees of enquiry, government departments and the politicians involved in the formulation of new laws and the legislative process. However, this approach can hardly be maintained in the light of the evidence from recent legislation. The connecting links between the two systems are extremely complex and require a more thorough elucidation than I have space for in this book. Yet, a number of facts are apparent even to the most unsophisticated observer. The first is that the police and Home Office together play a crucial part in controlling both the operation of the criminal justice process and the progress and direction of any proposals for reforming that process. To the Home Office and to successive Home Secretaries the maintenance of law and order in society has been synonymous with almost unquestioning support for the police and for the police the same objective is synonymous with the employment of coercive measures to deal with offenders and obtain convictions in the courts.

Secondly, it is surely a matter of some significance that in this country the government is able to control the appointment of judges and magistrates as well as being in a position to select the members of Royal Commissions and committees of enquiry set up to investigate aspects of the criminal justice system. One should add that in both cases the machinery of and criteria for selection are secret. However, the connection between the two systems does not merely consist of similarities between the sorts of people who are appointed to decision-making positions. There is also a remarkable concordance in the general style of administration. In both the criminal justice and law reform systems much attention is paid at the formal level to the principles of due process, neutrality, rationality and democracy. Much effort is spent in addressing both the criminal justice process and the law reform process with the rhetoric of these principles. Yet these rhetorical trappings only too often serve to conceal actions by state officials which have the effect of subverting these principles. In the police station, for example, the Judges' Rules serve as a symbol of the protection of the individual against police coercion, but in reality coercion has become part of everyday police practices. In the courtroom the rationality of the sentencing process and the neutrality of the sentencers are embodied in the formal legal framework, while that same framework allows magistrates and judges a free rein in projecting their values and prejudices in their sentencing decisions and to base such decisions on information about offenders which is highly selective and on occasions represents serious distortions of the facts. The independence of committees of enquiry and the selection of its members from all those who have an interest in its findings are widely respected as guiding principles, yet in the field of criminal justice such committees seem to be dominated by judiciary, the police and practising lawyers, while at the same time they appear to have only token representation or no representation at all from civil liberties organisations protecting the interests of defendants. Even in Parliament, the seat of democracy, the will of the democratically elected members may be subverted by skilful recourse to procedural rules and by the expedient use of the House of Lords.

This is not to suggest a sinister elitist conspiracy bent on the repression of individual rights and the undermining of democratic principles. What this gap between rhetoric and reality signifies is rather the prevalence of state paternalism, the belief predominant among many civil servants, senior politicians and members of the judiciary that they know what is best for the people of this country and that their knowledge and privileged position authorises them to take steps so as to protect people from themselves. This attitude, although less sinister than the notion of an elitist conspiracy, is none the less equally damaging in its effect on social institutions charged with maintaining the balance between the individual and the state. It is an attitude which gives rise to the belief that as long as the outward appearance of legality and democracy is maintained, it is perfectly legitimate to condone abuses and promote changes behind this facade. Taken to its extreme, anything may be justified just so long as one has the good of the people at heart.

To return to the starting point of this book, the main objection to the popular image of the criminal courts as places where battles between police and criminals are daily fought out according to the rules of law and the principles of justice is not that it leaves out so much of importance. It is rather that this image tends to blind people to the highly political nature of the criminal justice process by endowing that process with a mystique which sets it apart from other social events and institutions. At a somewhat more sophisticated level the study of the process as a system of rules has very much the same effect by treating events which concern the police and the courts as if they took place within a closed system isolated from those social forces which produce change and create resistance to change within our society. Even though studies of criminal justice which go beyond the level of formal rules and attempt to discover what actually happens in practice, behind the scenes, tend to take the formal rules as their starting point and to assess the behaviour of participants within the criminal justice system in terms of their conformity or non-conformity to the law or those expectations derived from their formal roles.[52]

All these approaches serve to enhance the notion of the criminal justice system as potentially rational and just, if only policemen, magistrates, lawyers and court clerks would behave themselves and obey the rules. Furthermore, they help to promote the notion that if things are wrong, then they can be put right simply by changing the rules. As bases for reform strategies, however, both these notions can have only very limited effectiveness. Much of the routinised behaviour which gives rise to complaints of rule-breaking is, as we have seen, the natural response of participants to pressures outside their control and outside the specific realm of criminal justice. As long as these pressures continue, so will the behaviour, whatever the rules may say. Changes in the rules will only serve to deflect that behaviour in other directions. Moreover, the rules themselves are often deliberately formulated in such a way as to permit the administrators of the system extensive free-

dom in their decision-making and this freedom is jealously guarded by
civil servants and by politicians in their efforts to resist change and to
ensure that power remains in the 'right' hands. Where changes are
permitted, they are allowed to occur only at a rhetorical level. Occasionally the facade of the system needs patching up, but behind that
facade things remain very much as they were.

Yet, I do not wish to end this book on a totally pessimistic note.
Recently new approaches to the study of law and legal institutions have
started to develop, their focus being the relationship between the law
and the state.[53] A number of recent studies have also attempted to
apply some of these theoretical concepts to aspects of the criminal
justice system as it has operated in specific historical concepts. These
have included a study of the response of the police and courts to the
Black riots in America[54] and to the phenomenon of mugging[55] in this
country. These studies have as their objective the understanding of the
law as it operates as part of a wider social system within particular
cultural, economic and political environments. With a very similar
objective in mind, I have taken a somewhat different approach in
this book by trying to expand the traditional conceptual framework
within which the criminal justice system is perceived and understood
and by using this expanded framework to analyse the system and explain its operations. Of course, understanding on its own does not produce change, although it may well be a step in the right direction.
What is, however, true is that the failure to understand is likely to
result in mis-spent energies, frustration and eventually total cynicism.
I hope this book will help prevent its readers from reaching this final
point of despair.

Notes

1. Cmnd. 4991 (HMSO, London, 1972).
2. M. King, *Bail or Custody* (Cobden Trust, London, 1971); s. Dell, *Silent in Court* (Bell, London, 1971); K. Bottomley, *Prison Before Trial* (Bell, London, 1970).
3. See Home Office Working Party, *Bail Procedures in Magistrates' Courts* (HMSO, London, 1974).
4. R. White, 'The Bail Act: Will it Make any Difference?' *Criminal Law Review* (1977), p. 339.
5. Home Office Report, *Bail Procedures,* para. 180.
6. Ibid., para 185.
7. H.O.C. No. 155, 1975 (CS18/75).
8. House of Lords, Debate 22.3.76. Hansard, col. 521.
9. Ibid., col. 520.

    10. House of Lords Debate 6.4.76. Hansard, col. 1530.
    11. Ibid., col. 1554.
    12. Ibid., col. 1586.
    13. House of Commons Debate 22.5.76. Hansard, cols. 512–514.
    14. Ibid., col. 534.
    15. Ibid., col. 487.
    16. Ibid., cols. 563 and 1551.
    17. Ibid., col. 517.
    18. Ibid., col. 517.
    19. House of Lords Debate 6.4.76. Hansard, col. 657.
    20. House of Commons Debate 26.3.76. Hansard, col. 546.
    21. House of Commons Debate 3.8.76. Hansard, col. 1547.
    22. *Criminal Statistics 1977–8, Prison Dept. Statistics 1975–8* (HMSO, London).
    23. Lord Justice James, (ch.) *The Distribution of Criminal Business between the Crown Court and Magistrates' Courts,* Cmnd. 6323 (HMSO, London, 1975).
    24. J. Gregory, *Crown Court or Magistrates' Court,* Social Survey (HMSO, London, 1976), p. 55.
    25. The James Committee's Report, p. 71.
    26. House of Lords Debate 10.2.77. Hansard, col. 1318.
    27. Ibid., col. 1317–8.
    28. Written Answers, 26.1.77. Hansard, col. 617–8.
    29. House of Lords Debate, 10.2.77. Hansard, col. 1317.
    30. Standing Committee on the Criminal Law Bill, 21.6.77. Hansard, col. 485.
    31. Ibid., col. 488.
    32. House of Lords Debate, 14.3.77. Hansard, col. 1373.
    33. Standing Committee, 21.6.77. Hansard, col. 474.
    34. Ibid., 28.6.77. Hansard, col. 615.
    35. Ibid., col. 623.
    36. Ibid., col. 628.
    37. House of Commons Debate, 13.7.77. Hansard, col. 496.
    38. Ibid., col. 506.
    39. Ibid.
    40. Ibid., col. 511.
    41. Ibid, col. 515.
    42. Ibid., col. 518.
    43. Ibid., col. 521.
    44. Ibid., col. 522.
    45. Ibid., col. 525.
    46. House of Lords Debate, 21.7.77. Hansard, col. 317.
    47. Ibid., col. 317.
    48. House of Commons Debate, 27.7.77. Hansard, col. 724.
    49. Ibid., col. 727.
    50. Ibid., col. 736.
    51. House of Commons Debate, 13.7.77. Hansard, col. 521.
    52. For a discussion of such reformist socio-legal studies see C. Cambell and P. Wiles, 'The Study of Law in Society in Britain', *Law and Society Review* (Summer 1976), pp. 547–77.
    53. I. Balbus, *The Dialectics of Legal Repression* (Russell Sage Foundation, New York, 1971), p. 4.
    54. Ibid.
    55. S. Hall, C. Critcher, T. Jefferson, J. Clarke and B. Roberts, *Policing the Crisis: Mugging, the State, Law and Order* (Macmillan, London, 1978).

Bibliography

Balbus, I. *The Dialectics of Legal Repression* (Russell Sage Foundation, New York, 1973)

Baldwin, J. 'The Compulsory Training of Magistrates', *Criminal Law Review* (1975), p. 634

—— 'Social Composition of the Magistracy', *British Journal of Criminology*, vol. 16, no. 2 (1976), pp. 171-4

—— and McConville, M. *Negotiated Justice* (Martin Robertson, London, 1977)

———— 'Police Interrogation and the Right to see a Solicitor', *Criminal Law Review* (1979), pp. 143-52

Bankowski, Z. and Mungham, G. *Images of Law* (Routledge and Kegan Paul, London, 1976)

Barnard, D. *The Criminal Court in Action* (Butterworths, London, 1974)

Bartlett, D. and Walker, J. 'Making Benches — The Inner Wheel', *New Society* (19 April 1973), p. 145

—— 'Wheel of Information', *New Society* (25 December 1975)

Bean, P. *Rehabilitation and Deviance* (Routledge and Kegan Paul, London, 1976)

Bedford, S. *The Faces of Justice* (Collins, London, 1961)

Benson, H. (chairman) *Report of the Royal Commission on Legal Services* (HMSO, London, 1979)

Bond, R. and Lemon, N. 'Changes in Magistrates' Attitudes during the First Year on the Bench', in Farrington, D. *et al.* (eds.), *Psychology. Law and Legal Processes* (Macmillan, London, 1978)

Bottoms, A.E. and McClean J.D. *Defendants in the Criminal Process* (Routledge and Kegan Paul, London, 1976)

Brown, J. *The Techniques of Persuasion* (Penguin, Harmondsworth, 1972)

Burney, E. *J.P. — Magistrate, Court and Community* (Hutchinson, London, 1979)

Cain, M. *Society and the Policeman's Role* (Routledge and Kegan

Paul, London, 1973)

Campbell, C. and Wiles, P. 'The Study of Law in Society in Britain', *Law and Society Review* (Summer 1976), pp. 547-77

Carlen, P. *Magistrates' Justice* (Martin Robertson, London, 1976)

Davies, C. 'The Innocent who Plead Guilty', *Law Guardian* (March 1970)

Davies, M. 'Social Enquiry Reports for the Courts', *British Journal of Criminology*, vol. 4 (1974), p. 18

Dell, S. *Silent in Court* (Bell, London, 1971)

Durkheim, E. *The Division of Labour in Society*, translated by G. Simpson (Macmillan, London, 1933)

Garfinkel, H. 'Conditions of Successful Degradation Ceremonies', *American Journal of Sociology*, vol. 6 (1956), pp. 420-4 Gifford, T.

Gifford, T. and O'Connor, P. 'Habeas Corpus', *Legal Action Group Bulletin* (1979), p. 182

Glazer, B. and Strauss, A. *Status Passage* (Routledge and Kegan Paul, London, 1971)

Griffiths T., 'Ideology in Criminal Procedure or A Third Model of the Criminal Process', *The Yale Law Journal*, vol. 79, no. 3. (1970), pp. 359-417.

Hadden, T. and Hillyard, P. *Justice in Northern Ireland* (Cobden Trust, London, 1973)

Hall, S. *et al. Policing the Crisis: Muggings, the State and Law and Order,* (Macmillan, London, 1978)

Hine, J., McWilliams, W. and Pease, K. 'Recommendations, Social Information and Sentencing', *Howard Journal*, vol. 17 (1978), pp. 91-100

Home Office Working Party, *Bail Procedures in Magistrates' Courts* (HMSO, London, 1974)

Hood, R. *Sentencing in Magistrates' Courts* (Stevens, London, 1962)

— — *Sentencing the Motoring Offender* (Heinemann, London, 1972)

Ingelby, O. (chairman) *Report of the Committee on Children and Young Persons,* Cmnd. 1191 (HMSO, London, 1960)

James, Lord Justice (chairman) *The Distribution of Criminal Business between the Crown Court and Magistrates' Courts,* Cmnd. 6323 (HMSO, London, 1975)

Kadish, S. and Paulson, M. *Criminal Law and its Processes,* 3rd edn (Little Brown, Boston, USA, 1975)

King, M. *Bail or Custody* (Cobden Trust, 1971)

— — (ed.) *Guilty until Proved Innocent* (Release Lawyers, London, 1973)

—— 'Magistrates' Courts Surveyed', *Rights,* vol. 1, no. 1 (1976), p. 11

—— *Duty Solicitors* (Cobden Trust, London, 1976)

—— 'A Status Passage Analysis of the Defendant's Progress through the Magistrates' Court', *Law and Human Behaviour,* vol. 2, no. 3 (1978), p. 211

Laurie, P. *Scotland Yard* (Penguin, Harmondworth, 1972)

Levinson, H. 'Legal Aid in Summary Proceedings in Magistrates' Courts Revisited', *New Law Journal* (1979), p. 375

Lukács, G. *History and Class Consciousness* (Merlin Press, London, 1971)

Packer, H. *The Limits of the Criminal Sanction* (Stanford University Press, Stanford, USA, 1969)

Perry, F. *Information for the Courts—A New Look at Social Inquiry Reports* (Cambridge Institute for Criminology, Cambridge, 1974)

Rheinstein, M. (ed.) *Max Weber on Law and Economy in Society* (Harvard Unversity Press, Cambridge, USA, 1954)

Royal Commission on the Selection of Justices of the Peace, *Report,* Cmnd. 2865 (HMSO, London, 1910)

Simon, F. and Weatheritt, M. *The Use of Bail and Custody by London Magistrates Before and After the Criminal Justice Act 1967* (HMSO, London, 1974)

Shapland, J. 'The Construction of a Mitigation', in Farrington, D. *et al.* (eds.) *Psychology, Law and Legal Processes* (Macmillan, London, 1978)

Streatfield, G.H.B. (chairman) *Report of the Interdepartmental Committee on the Business of the Criminal Courts,* Cmnd. 1289 (HMSO, London, 1962)

Sudnow. D. 'Normal Crimes', *Social Problems,* vol. 12 (Winter 1965), pp. 225–75

Tarling, R. *Sentencing Practice in Magistrates' Courts. Home Office Research Study no. 56* (HMSO, London, 1979)

Thomas, D. *Principles of Sentencing,* 2nd edn (Heinemann, London, 1979)

Thorpe, J. *Social Enquiry Reports* (HMSO, London, 1979)

Widgery, Lord Justice (chairman), *Report of the Departmental Committee on Legal Aid in Criminal Proceedings,* Cmnd. 2934 (HMSO, London, 1966)

White, R. 'The Bail Act, Will it Make Any Difference?', *Criminal Law Review* (1977), p. 339

White, S. 'Homilies in Sentencing', *Criminal Law Review* (1971), p.690

—— 'The Presentation in Court of Social Inquiry Reports', *Criminal*

Law Review (1971), p. 629

Zander, M. 'Access to a Solicitor in the Police Station', *Criminal Law
    Review* (1972), p. 342

Index